ANCHOR
BOOKS

EXPRESSIONS FROM SCOTLAND, IRELAND & WALES 2005

Edited by

Sarah Marshall

First published in Great Britain in 2005 by
ANCHOR BOOKS
Remus House,
Coltsfoot Drive,
Peterborough, PE2 9JX
Telephone (01733) 898102

SB ISBN 1 84418 387 4

FOREWORD

Anchor Books is a small press, established in 1992, with the aim of promoting readable poetry to as wide an audience as possible.

We hope to establish an outlet for writers of poetry who may have struggled to see their work in print.

The poems presented here have been selected from many entries, and as always editing proved to be a difficult task.

I trust this selection will delight and please the authors and all those who enjoy reading poetry.

Sarah Marshall
Editor

CONTENTS

BIDED MY TIME

And this is the very moment
I've been biding my time for
In this very instant
I know that I love you
Never thought I could feel so elated
You make all so possible
Thought all of my yesterdays were worthless
But not when they've led me to you
And I'm hoping to get two tomorrows
For every yesterday I've endured alone
Although each day I find your arms around me
Never want tomorrow but for today to never end
And with a gladdened heart I smile
Relishing the life we're gonna spend together
Trusting I can prove successful
Letting you know you mean everything to me.

Elaine Donaldson

MY ISLE

As summer day draws to an end,
When cool of evening does descend.
Swallows dart through still night air
All is at peace, and without care.
The evening sun sinks down to die
To leave a pink and crimson sky,
Shadows over land then creep,
Night will bring its silent sleep.

That precious hour is now at hand,
When eyes behold a mystic land,
A place of beauty, so sublime
Yet still untouched by pass of time.
High mountains with their bubbling streams
Make music, heard within my dreams,
While birds around their summits soar
And waves crash, on that distant shore.

As daylight ebbs and fades away
With heavy heart these words I pray
Just give me but one moment more
To savour all, that I adore.
The darkness falls, my dream is gone
Now I must wait until the dawn,
To end this night so long and barren
Then to return, my Island, Arran.

I A Morrison

I CAN

I can write a poem,
For anyone who'd ask,
I don't want food nor money,
Or whisky from your hip flask.

I can write a poem
With an insight of who you are,
From the clothes you wear and if
You care for the environment and have no car.

I like to write a poem,
Especially if I know,
The secrets you keep, when you sleep
To help my writing flow.

If you'd let me write a poem,
Don't tell me when to stop,
So I keep the flow, for you to know
That your one sounds just top.

Ian Dunne

GIRL

The very thought of you arouses all my senses.
Thy beauty far greater than would befit a princess.

At first sight, the big bang, the birth of time anew.
How it all began, I still haven't got a clue.

Thy sculpted body, a mountain landscape the river carves.
Thy dark mane, a cascade adorning thy back's stately curves.

Thy face, the radiant sun and merciful moon rolled into one.
Thy eyes, sparkling with the shimmer of stars a million.

Thy slender limbs, gleaming white as winter snow.
Thy silky skin, set ablaze by sunset's golden glow.

Thy green veins, like tendrils entwining a tender stem.
Thy palms so pink, are roses in full bloom held by them?

Thy sensuous lips, strawberries offering a sumptuous delight.
Thy cheeks had Eve possessed, Satan would have taken the bite.

Thy hidden inner beauty, vast treasures the jungles conceal.
Thy forbidden secrets yet unfound, will thou to me reveal?

Watching thee in thy soft slumber, still as a placid lake.
With the sun's first rays bouncing off thy gold-rimmed
silhouette, I awake.

Thy fragrance, reminiscent of a stroll through the garden path.
Drawn unto thy flame of passion, I am the moth.

Thy voice beckons to me, a sparrow echoing through the valley.
Won't you, oh! nightingale, sing thy song just for me?

Thou feed me like a mother would, a child from her womb.
Thou heal me like time would mend a sore wound.

In a shower of joy, you join me for a dance in the rain.
In the tempest of despair, you offer solace and soothe the pain.

Thy laughter, sweet timbre of scattered pearls.
Thy smile, a rainbow encompassing both worlds.

Thy touch, a soft caress of the cool evening breeze.
Thy hug, a warm embrace of a mountain mist engulfing the trees.

Thy kiss, a splash of waves crashing on the beach.
Thy love, oh! Wonders of the Universe within my reach.

When thou leave me for a while, I feel blue as the empty sky.
Leave me forever, the void, a black hole, the end of time. Goodbye.

Thy femme form, a mere ten thousand years of age.
In Nature's billion year history, you are but a page.

When the real Nature's bounty lies bare, true for all to see,
Oh, girl of my dreams, why am I wasting my time with thee?

Prasad Rajendran

A CANDLE FLAME

I burn but brief
Maybe for grief
I burn for hope
Maybe to cope

But my heart's desire
is to inspire . . .

Look into my flame
Encompass my heart
I struggle just the same
Serve my purpose then depart

I burn to light
To put things right
I am a fire
Your heart's desire

To illuminate
would serve me great

I serve to remember
All things tender
Look at me and hope
Then you will cope.

Mary Shovlin

WHAT HAS HAPPENED TO OUR WORLD?

This world was created many years ago,
It was made out of love by God above
He made many beautiful things,
Just like the little birds that often sing.

God made me and you but can we do?
This world was made out of love
Now it's being destroyed through hatred and war.
What has happened to our world?
What are they trying to score?

Many people take drugs and fight
What can we do with all God's love and might
To just put this world just right?

So many innocent lives being destroyed
By war and violence on our streets
What can we do to put that smile back on our cheeks
And avoid the many cries we often meet when on our streets?

Doesn't anyone care out there
Or are they just willing to bare the suffering and pain?
What does one gain by giving others so much pain?

What has happened to our world?
Does anyone know? I don't think so.
Does the government care about the lives out there,
Killings, blood shed?
What are they going to do?
Wait until most of us are laid to rest too.

Anastasia Williams Cowper

UNIVERSITY

She's off to university,
there she goes,
all grown up
from her head to her toes.

On the motorway,
car all full,
all grown up
it's not gonna be dull.

She's got a lotta stuff,
all going with her,
all grown up
there's no time for me, urgh.

Getting in her room,
wow what a sight,
all grown up
sleeping there tonight.

Will it all fit in?
Pens and safety pins,
all grown up
unpacking all her things.

Meeting new friends,
from all around,
all grown up
new things to be found.

Starting all her lessons,
there's learning to do,
all grown up
there's work for you.

We're leaving her behind,
no more music in our ear
all grown up
we miss her, she's there, we're here.

Jade E Taylor (10)

THE RAINBOW OF LIFE

Red is the vibrant colour of life
As we go through those childhood years
Symbolising the voyage of great discovery
When we have no worries, or fears

Orange is the dawn of maturity
When our minds turn to other things
We realise, those stories of birds and bees
Didn't just mean they have wings

Yellow represents the gradual calming
As our impetuous youth is left behind
The responsibilities of adult life
Are suddenly impressed on our mind

Green is the natural abundance of life
When our young crop is growing up, fast
We see in them, what we used to have
And we pray, that their happiness will last

Blue is the period of thinking back
When we spend all our time, reminiscing
We enviously watch the emerging youth
And rue the good times, which we're missing

Indigo is the dusk of our lifelong day
We relax, from all anguish, and strife
Giving each other the love, which we'll need
For the impending sunset of life

Violet is the end of our lifelong year
We finally meet the cold of December
But we leave behind us, a rainbow of colours
Which we hope that our young will remember.

Eric Twist

ROLLER COASTERS AND TOFFEE APPLES

(In memory of Albert)

Lengthy car journeys, playing games, singing songs,
Finding the odd one out, placing it where it belongs,
How many red cars and how many blue?
Joining the dots with 'Winnie the Pooh'
Eating pear drops that come out of a tin,
Filled with joy, waiting for the fun to begin.
'Are we there yet?' comes the familiar call,
'Not yet, I'm afraid'
'Will we get there at all?'
Roads stretching out in the distance, so long,
'Come along let's sing another car song,'
Ten green bottles still sitting on the wall,
Waiting again for a number to fall.
Reading Enid Blyton and starting to feel sick,
Staring straight ahead, 'Will that do the trick?'
Feeling better now and look, I can see . . .
Golden sand and candyfloss stretching out before me,
Roller coasters, toffee apples and the smell of fish and chips,
I can remember quite distinctly the taste of salt on my lips,
Buckets and spades, windbreakers and deck chair,
The feeling of the sea breeze as it blows through my hair,
Shells and pebbles and the green seaweed that pops,
Wearing a floppy sun hat with swimsuit and flip-flops,
'Can we have ice cream?'
'No, not before tea, perhaps a bit later, we'll just have to see.'
I can still hear the sea in the shells that I took,
And I remember the stories in the Enid Blyton book,
The memories are as magic as the holidays we had,
Bringing a smile to my face and making me glad.

Annie Morrice

DESTINY
(Dedicated to Aled)

When you're searching for your destiny,
Remember don't look back.
Even though many tears may fall,
And you feel your heart might crack,
You can only face forward,
In your dreams to start anew.

Going back in time is never easy
And will make you sad and blue,
Open your eyes to the many wonders,
That you alone can survey.
This is what you've been hoping for,
At the start of each new day!

Mary 'Storm' George

THE SANITARY MAN

I remember in my younger days
We had very scant hygiene
Yet comparing this in those modern times
It always seemed so clean.

Most dogs were kept in kennels
Where their droppings lay around
So their owners found it easy
To clean this soiled ground.

Then there was a day in the week
When a pig-breeder would appear,
He collected food scraps people laid out
For the young pigs that he reared.

Next came the rag and bone men
Who collected metals and old rags
Who gave you a cup and saucer
If you helped to fill their bags.

Most newspapers all were burned
With some trimmed up for the loo
There were no signs of plastic bags
Which today is the refuse man's taboo.

Shopkeepers all used newspapers
To wrap their customers goods
You didn't need a safe cracker
To retrieve your wrapped up food.

The local councils have a section
Called the Environmental Plan
When all that was provided years ago
Was a good Sanitation man.

Lachlan Taylor

OUR LOVE

Our love cannot be compared,
To that of mortal existence,
Our passion shall never remit,
For it's heavenly in its brilliance.

Our love is a oneness of being,
With romantic benevolence herewith,
Our blood of mysterious union,
Pumps furiously among loving bliss.

Our love lies deep inside,
Resident in each other's heart,
Exploding the flames of desire,
An inferno to banish the dark.

Our love will never be challenged,
Never forgotten, nor passed,
Our bonding of timeless beauty,
As infinite in the joy it has cast.

Paul Mackenzie

LESSON OF THE WAVES

That great seabird-assassin, the skua,
leaves the fulmars and kittiwakes fewer,
most of whom don't deserve
to end up as hors d'oeuvres
or, recycled, as guano (manure).

It's a thug and a pain in the ass.
If the gulls got together en masse
with collectivist will
they could counter its kill
and its bloated consumption would pass.

Norman Bissett

BOYS AND GIRLS COME OUT TO PLAY

The golden days of childhood are the sweetest ones of all
Running, playing, skipping in the summer or the fall
I'm sure you all have seen a child, who skips from side to side
This golden magic movement makes my heart to open wide

The freest day of men or women, childhood days divine
The heart is young and open, fresh air flows down like wine
No reason to feel happy just run and catch the wind
Boys and girls come out to play, let us now begin

When your body starts to falter and it's hard to get about
To catch your breath you stop a while, it's true without a doubt
A child skips by, cries, 'Hello', it makes you young again
You turn and wave and smile at them, forgetting all your pain

For though the years have took their toll upon your body's meld
Deep inside a child still lives, life's candle still is held
You cannot run or skip about but light up when you ee
Children playing all around, their joy lights up you ee.

For I'll go out and play again when life's toil is o'er
My spirit will be free to skip above this mortal core
Young and fresh and free again I'll run upon the grass
A child again on Heaven's shore, I shall be free at last.

Roy A Millar

I WILL BE THERE FOR YOU

Let me be the one to hold your hand in mine
When things get you down
Let me be the one who wipes away your tears
When I hear you weeping aloud,
Let me be the one with whom you can confide
When times are hard
Let me be the one who listens to your voice
When you are in a crowd.

Let me be the one to share your dreams
When they seem impossible
Let me be the one to cast away your doubts
When times trouble you,
Let me be the one to share your misfortune
As you would mine
Let me be the one to help you smile again
When you are feeling blue.

Let me be the one to take away your pain
When you are suffering so
Let me be the one to guide you through darkness
When you see no light,
Let me be the one who understands you for you
When others judge you wrongly
Let me be the one who loves you all the more
When day becomes night.

George S Johnstone

NUMB . . .

Sorrow is like heavy chains
Locked and wrapped tightly around my fragile heart.
Binding me, crushing my hopes and dreams,
Rendering me without a care of life, left numb!

Pam McCormack

SENSES

A thought, a dream, a sigh, a breath full deep.
Eyes meet, hearts melt, senses sleep, the fruit the nostrils reap.
Love on the light rays, foliage in trepidation.
Smoky visual opera, soft calmness of the nation.

Tender music, clothed in colour, sweet and right,
Image of splendour, drunk with peace, flock in flight.
Sounds of shyness, childlike meekness, mild applause.
Seen amid a room of passion and ticking time,
This moment of completeness, the moment's mine.

Kind smiles and dual acceptance, the fragrance keen,
Views of travel through the brain, of sun and sea,
A field afar, a land of love, a place for you and me,
Tomorrow when the world is wise, we'll laugh and we'll be free.

Patrick Martin

COME WITH ME ON A JOURNEY

Will you come with me on a journey?
Will you stay with me and see it through?
But please don't ask me any questions
Because those questions will be revealed to you.

Will you trust me and do everything I say?
Will you do everything I ask of you?
Will you follow me through all the barriers
That will face us as time passes, to the new?

Follow me now as our journey begins
Take in everything that you see and hear.
I am only your guide and teacher
It is the knowledge that will question your fear.

Niall McManus

PROPAGATION

May the propagation
Of Cape primrose
or Streptocarpus be
prodigious.
These flowers look prestigious
and lovely.

They have been
blooming in my room
for nearly three months, and the
donor of the flower
Margaret Mavor
monitors the
flower's behaviour
when she visits me;
(but the first flower
now hangs her head).
Two severed leaves in earth
await birth;
one
has been given
to a green fingered nun.
I would like to
leave a leaf
of my personality
with a relative or friend who
could propagate it - sort of
similarly.

Valerie Faith Irvine-Fortescue

DAMNED HEART

I call to thee, my constant ache,
this fervour which doth conquer me.
I damn this heart, lest thou forsake,
I beseech thee torment, set me free.
Upon this hour thy soul shall bleed,
thine eyes behold no worthy heart.
As I speak, pay thine ears no heed,
for no sweet thing doth my lips impart.
My head this fervour doth confuse;
Nailed firm betwixt my heart and head,
this love doth my damned heart abuse,
and wails the tune of pain instead.
So I call to thee, my constant woe,
and damn this heart, till love bestow.

Laura Laird

TO FRIENDS

Don't look too far inside of me
you might not like it when you see,
the close-knit web of different lives,
the violent calm, the compromise,
of complex masks that gild the eyes,
the hurtful truth, the violent lies,
depressive thoughts, oppressive sighs,
of anger, hurt and hate that cries
out - *leave me be I need you.*

Don't dig too deep inside of me,
you will not like it when you see,
the rotten cards life dealt there;
the bitter hate, the loving care
of animals, but not mankind, for fear
that they should pry and hear
the vengeful death that I will bear
to all who cross me, for I should sear
apart - *rather than you pity me.*

Don't force your way inside of me,
you may be frightened when you see,
the things I have in store for you,
days of peace, days when blue,
thoughts that waken with the dew,
and rise in turmoil confused and new,
that cannot meet the coming morn and rue
the day that they were born, and grew
angrily so - *go away I need you.*

Leigh Crighton

DUNFERMLINE'S GRAVES

Behind this church-like fortress
Lies the strength of a maiden's honour
I cowl and shudder

Under the breath of a cold icy wind
Hunting in packs of fog.
The freezing gusts rattle my sleep
For no blood do I have
To keep the bones in check.

Silent warriors stand guard
Over this home of mine
Whispers are the new bells
Tulips their mass of colour

As I rest
I hear the padded feet of mourners
Their souls intact wailing fiercely
Another Clansman
To go forth to kneel
In front of The Almighty
His hunger knows no bounds.

Souls await the full moon
The guiding light
To Celestial Heaven
Coldness at night
Leaves no time for thought

Honesty betrayed by greed
Tea leaves swirl in a cup
Stained by misadventure

Bruce awaits his call
Brass be his solid stance
Awaiting a silent game.

Anton Nicholas

LOOKING BACK

Looking back on my life I wonder how it would have been
Would I still be lying here if I had stayed clean?
Would I have stolen from my family?
Would I have broken my mother's heart?
Would I have ended up in prison if I had never let this start?
Would my skin be dull and lifeless?
Would my teeth rot in my head?
Would I still look like I'm sixty, when I'm thirty and nearly dead?
Did I think of all these factors with the needle in my arm?
Was the buzz and the sensation really worth the harm?
Why did I choose the gutter when I had a nice warm bed at home?
Why did I help to make the dealers rich and end up all alone?
It's too late for me to wonder, my time on Earth is done,
Just another statistic *don't let them make you one!*

Maureen Quinn

MAGICAL KISS . . .

Just one kiss
Is all it took from your tender lips . . .
My heart pounding with excitement
Adrenaline pumping through every inch of my body
Eagerly awaiting the second kiss . . .
Mixed feelings of passion and wonder
What are these feelings?
Never before have I felt such confusion . . .
Was this love I was feeling?
The love I have searched for all my life
Yet had failed for all my tries . . .
Love, to set my heart on fire
Like a volcano erupting with passion and desire . . .
From the core of my soul I lust for more
You are the key to my heart
You have unlocked my door . . .

Janet Brook

LINLITHGOW

Night falls on Lithgow loch waters,
Silver to satin to steel.
Darkness enfolds the Palace
Where shadows writhe and weave.
An opal moon sheds a pearly light
And the wind plays a pavanne in the trees.

The King salutes his lady,
Courtiers watch jewel-eyed,
The ensemble steps into the Great Hall
To measure a gay galliard.
The viols are perfectly silent.
The flambeaus give out no light.
The banquet has rotted and crumbled
For all of the dancers have died.

When grey fingers signal the morning
The spectres bow and depart.
Memories fade into the stonework,
Cobbles lie quiet in the yard.
Gauze Mist drifts over the marshes
Wild geese sarabande in the light.

Barbara Hammond

TWEEDDALE LANDMARKS

Neidpath Castle, Neidpath Castle,
Neidpath Castle by Tweed's dark river,
Scene of many a Border foray,
Theme of many a poet's lay.
River music, river music,
From the waters flowing by you,
Shining silver in the starlight,
Sparkling in the sun by day.

Glentress Forest, Glentress Forest,
Glentress Forest with glades enchanting,
Bright with foxgloves in their season,
Ringed by oak and beech and larch.
Mossy pathways, mossy pathways,
Where it is a joy to wander,
Where across the whispering streamlets,
Birches form a shadowy arch.

Hill of Cademuir, Hill of Cademuir,
Hill of Cademuir with slopes of bracken,
Or with swathes of glorious heather,
Through which flows an amber stream.
Airy summit, airy summit,
Whence I view the Manor valley,
And the ridges that surround it,
Scene as lovely as a dream.

E Margaret Kidd

HINDSIGHT HAIKU

Looking back, knowledge
Emerged from questing and
From struggle, wisdom.

Unforgiving, then,
Of our parents; patient, now
With our dear children.

W A Boden

Rubha Nam Brathairean

finding a new place is always good
so what
if big uggy and the guys checked it out
thousands of years ago
it's new to me
(i've been a virgin many times)

the strange thing in this case was
i walked right past it
went on down to the shore
i noticed the rusting rear end of a 1960's mini
picked up on the gaze of a querulous sheep
so close it showed me the mountains reflected in its eyes

i took pictures of rocks
sat by a little waterfall
thought about what i'd say to an old love
wished for other things
to preserve the moment
a fire
a friend
a guitar
a bottle

then
a few introspective minutes later
i set off up the steep pathway
almost back at the road
there
on the other side of a drystone wall
i saw a tombstone
a single granite syllable against the sky

cryogenics seemed superfluous
this place
and
these intangible names and spirits
were perfectly preserved
still a part of their own environment
watched over by what they had loved

then i saw the new gateway
an angular galvanised monstrosity
an intrusive alien
in a pantheistic landscape

who put that thing here
why not a wooden gate
i stood there
quietly fuming
wanting to defend the dead

slowly
so slowly
i became aware of sound
a plaintive keening
picking up the echoes of the stones

there in that abomination of an entrance
holes had been drilled
perhaps by some machine
pre-programmed
to prepare for fitments never fitted

yet now
each hole had purpose
each one an aeolian embouchure

playing an improvised last post
with pitch and tone
rubato slurs
chosen by the changing wind

when i go - as all must go
bury me where the breezes blow.

V J Roberts

CLOUDS

Clouds at night, move slow,
Past a triangle of glass,
A window,
To view a screening,
A private screening just for me,
The clouds I see form shapes,
Of faces, animals, wraiths,
Sentient beings, they never rest,
Magical moment, timing like a dream,
I am hypnotised for a while,
As they smile at me,
Like a familiar friend,
Floating between land and sky,
They hint at Heaven.

William Lightheart

FALSE SMILES

False smiles are what I seem to get from people
                                pretending to be my friends.
Their smiles go right to their ears, telling me everything
                                            I want to hear.
How long do they think it will take me to see all the
                                hidden intentions waiting for me?
For very few people I have met that will do things for me
                                        that have no benefits
So all you people with your fake smiles so twisted and cruel
Keep on smiling cos I am nobody's fool.
It has come to the day so sad and true, that trying to find
human faith is more like the lottery pool, you never know
what you are going to get, the golden jackpot or Satan's best friend.
So keep your wits about you when choosing a friend,
Cause there is very few that will stay with you to the end.

Clare Lithgow

CATCH ME IF YOU CAN

Tammy trout was swimming aboot
The river was home his only route
Up and down he swam every day
Wallowing in weather come what may

At weekends many anglers came past
With rods in hand their lines to cast
The banks and rocks were his to confuse
Out of the sunlight lures he would refuse

The bait they offered tempted him not
For hide and seek was all they got
Many years ago he learned how to swim
Now you know there are no flies on him!

The flowing stream for him to breed
A future ahead for life to proceed
A fishy story is all that one can say
So zip up your fly and make my day.

Norman S Brittain

THE LIFE OF THE MONARCH

Dae' ye mind o' Billy Connick,
　　The Monarch o' the Glen,
Who sometimes made a penny,
　　for a wee dram noo an' then.

Weel, the pennies soon were shillin's,
　　An' the shillin's soon were pounds,
For he had got ambitions,
　　and ambition kens' nae bounds.

His wife was little better,
　　she had the same disease,
There was nae opportunity,
　　she didna' try to sieze.

They sailed forth on pleasure,
　　an' traivelled near an' far
an' aye they had a notion,
　　to own a motor car.

She started up in business,
　　an' set hersel's a task,
To make a little fortune,
　　but how! Ye dinna' ask.

They soon amassed a tidy sum,
　　to slap doon as deposit,
They said they saved it honestly,
　　but honestly! Now was it?

Some day they're gaun tae buy a hoose,
　　an' move oot o' their garret,
She'll hae tae hire a maid or twa,
　　an' he'll have to hae a valet.

She'll be the lady o' the town,
     wi' velvet, silks and mink,
an' whaur the money comes from,
     wad gar' a body think.

The bairns'll learn to ride a horse,
     they'll enter for the show,
'that's my daughters at the front,'
     you'll hear auld Maggie crow.

She'll sit beside the Monarch,
     in their fancy motor car,
She'll drink the gin and tonic,
     while he smokes a fat cigar.

Till one day the Tax Man comes,
     an' asks them wi' a sob,
To tak' him on as chauffeur,
     he was desperate for a job.

Tammy D

LIMERICKS

Our new local postman is glum,
Saying dog owners, mostly, are scum,
I just saw him today,
Running every which way,
With a terrier clamped on his bum.

An avid young rambler called Grace,
Found herself in an out of bounds place,
She just laughed at the sign,
Then she trod on a mine,
And left without leaving a trace.

A dirty old crofter called Nell,
Thought that sleeping with pigs would be swell,
So she tried it one day,
But the pigs ran away,
They just couldn't put up with the smell.

A man called Lee, ran off to sea,
To escape from his nagging wife,
As he sailed with the tide,
He fell over the side
And lay dead for the rest of his life.

Mattew L Burns

DADS NEED CUDDLES

I know it always seems to you
I am the one that shouts
But my love for you is just as strong
Of this, please have no doubts,
Your mother's here to comfort you
And wipe away your tears,
But I'm always in your corner
To chase away your fears
I know your cuddles are special
Between your mum and you,
But please try to remember
That dads need cuddles too.

T Elliott

SUMMER BREEZE

As the evening emerges and heaves a great yawn.
The night life awakes to work hard until dawn.
Dark shadows transpire conifers that silhouette the night sky.
A summer breeze hits the senses and stops one being wry.
Moments like this are second to none;
Moments like this without starlight or sun.
For a brief moment you stand there alone;
yet you know deep within that you're not on your own.
All this evokes the beginning of time -
when the life on this planet was so very sublime.

Darryl Kristan Benson

GETTING IT RIGHT

While on a trip to Whitley Bay
During the merry month of May,
I saw a shepherd on a rock
Keeping a watch over his flock.

Sheep form a flock, never a herd,
So shepherd is a stupid word;
And then this thought entered my head:
I'd call him a shep-flock instead!

Roger Williams

MY HIGHLAND HOME

Rising in the morning,
As the dawn begins to break,
I'd step outside my drystane croft,
A deep breath I would take,

The dew would sparkle on the grass,
With snow high on the hill.
The sweet scent of the heather,
The air is cool and still.

In the distance, I would see,
A herd of roaming deer,
Whilst overhead a sudden cry,
An eagle would appear,

Soaring o'er the mountains,
Searching for his prey,
His screams so melancholy
He passes on his way.

Water with a thunderous roar,
Falls down the mountainside,
Giving off a vapour,
As little creatures hide.

There is a feeling in my heart,
My spirits seem to fly.
From this place I'll never part,
It's here that I would die.

No other place in this wide world,
I'd ever care to roam,
I have all I need right here,
In my Glen Coe Home.

T Bradley

THIS WILL PUT A THISTLE UP YER KILT

One day O'Grady
Was approached by an upper class lady,
The lady was rather arty-crafty,
As she said to O'Grady the dafty,
'Could you paint me in the nude?'
Said O'Grady, 'Don't think me rude
But I'd rather keep my socks on,'
This will put a thistle up yer kilt.

One day the vicar's wife,
Rebuked O'Grady for his wife,
For the umpteen kids he fathered,
'Your sins will all have gathered,'
O'Grady said, 'Not on yer life,
See my trouble and strife,'
This will put a thistle up yer kilt.

One day O'Grady backed a horse,
And it won of course,
Now all that champagne
Has went and rotted his brain
'The richest man in Ireland is insane',
Read The Sun headline again,
O'Grady showed his disdain
By backing another winner,
Now he's invited the queen round for dinner,
This will put a thistle up yer kilt.

Alan Pow

WISDOM

Wisdom said to the heart
'Be firm and strong
For when you meet sorrowful days
And the days of utter joy
You will buckle under them both
If you don't hold firm and strong.

Look at my calm!
When I meet worldly woes
And see the days of sheer bliss,
My words lessen the woes
And enhance the day's bliss.'

Heart pondered!
And said to Wisdom,
'You are what you are
And I am what I am

You may be firm and strong
But when I see tears in a child's eyes
And bloodshed needlessly,
I cannot help but ache
And bleed with sorrow.

When I see fragrant love
And smell sweet scent of flowers,
Like a sentimental fool in love
I melt with immense joy.'

A Jamil

RUMOUR MACHINE

We live in a town where gossip is rife,
Where the rumour machine is part of our life,
It doesn't take much to set it in motion,
Idle talk blown out of proportion.

People in shops, in the pubs and the clubs,
They feed the machine its favourite grub,
It's gossip it needs as it gathers momentum,
Like some giant sea creature devouring plankton.

The rumour machine can ruin a life,
The misery, the heartache, the trouble, the strife,
The gossip mongers keep peddling their wares,
The snide remarks, the vacant stares.

It's par for the course in such a small place,
Where suspicion is cast on every new face,
No one is safe from the dreaded machine,
The vicar, the Judge, not even the Queen.

Willard Griffiths

A Peaceful Scene

The sky was beautiful this morning
Just as the day was dawning.
Clouds akin to feathery plumes,
Roses still in full bloom.
Fine rain is trickling down,
Clearing the air all around.
Rabbits scampering here and there,
Now and again they stop and stare.
So peaceful here - only the twittering of the birds
In the branches of the trees is to be heard.
Up above the drone of a plane flying past
Breaking the silence which sadly did not last -
Grey now is the scene with a hint of blue
So I shall go indoors as I have much to do.

Gwyneth Scott

TO THE MACMILLAN NURSES

What would we do without these wonderful girls,
They nurse cancer patients from all over the world.
Though they know their patients are passing away
They devote their time with them for little pay.

Their reward is the thanks from the families and friends
Of all the thousands of patients they have to attend.
It must be heartbreaking at times I am sure
When they did their best but could do no more.

Cancer we know is a terrible disease,
It is not something we can accept with ease.
Only those who have it can really know
How it fills your life with fear and woe.

Then along comes a MacMillan nurse with a smile
Ready to make life happier for one, if just for a while.
They give you courage and help to ease the pain
So you look forward to their visit again.

They comfort and guide you through the path you must go,
These angels of mercy who love their work so.
They deserve all the help we can possibly give
For the help they give to others, who have not long to live.

Phyllis Ing

HANNAH'S LIFE IN A POEM

One year after January 1989,
A little girl, Hannah, was born so divine.
Long wavy hair upon her head,
'She looks like an angel,' was repeatedly said.

Nothing ever made her cry,
She always smiled, my oh my.
Her mother hugged her always tight,
Until she dropped her one awful night!

Hannah fell onto the floor,
And smacked her head on the door.
'It was an accident,' screamed the mother
As the father worried, 'Oh brother!'

The nurse took Hannah to intensive care,
The mum was confused and asked her, 'Where?'
Tests were done and blood was taken
When Hannah awoke her head was aching!

'We have bad news,' explained the nurse,
The mother cried and clutched her purse
And ever since Hannah hit her head hard,
She has always been a stupid retard!

Hannah Buck

DESTINY'S WIND

(For Amanda - a treasured friend)

My sails are set to catch destiny's wind
Taking me to a new land
From where I'll reach out and take your hand
And place in it a loving wish
For you and those I cherish
And I'll send my love
On the wings of a dove
And in amidst the falling rain
I'll plant kisses to help ease your pain
And from your side I will not be far
Just look to the sky and I'll be the first evening star
Helping to light your way
And at the end of the day
I will be but a thought away.

Jan Maissen

His Toy Lamb

I noticed a young girl pushing a pram,
Inside a boy with his toy lamb.
Every night he took it to bed,
White fleeced, felt eared, with rounded head.
The child and lamb were closely bond,
He clutched it for he was very fond -
At Christmas, a lamb in Christ's manger there,
And with it his own he did compare.
Sadly the day his sorrow began,
His favourite toy was lost from the pram.
Shaken from the blanket the young girl tossed,
Afraid to admit her careless loss.
Her boyfriend laughed, 'Have no regret.
He's only five, he'll soon forget.'
A memory he never forsook,
There was a lamb in his picture book.
He dreams of Christ's manger in his sleep,
Finds his lamb with the shepherds' sheep.
Wonderfully peaceful were his dreams,
Friendship, children and beautiful scenes.
He woke to birdsong and gentle rain,
The hawthorn flowering in the lane.
Soon summer - hum of the honeybee,
The sun, the beach, white flecked the sea.
Flush autumn berries, the staghorn flame,
Hardly a tree with leaves remain.
Later comes Christmas on his mind,
Into the hedgerow a secret find!
Attracted by the traveller's joy,
I saw the girl lift up the boy
To the old man's beard above their heads,
His fingers touched, 'My lamb,' he said.

A E Doney

ARE YOU THE ONE?

Are you the one who will always hold me dear,
protect me from all evil and all that I will fear?

Are you the one who will hold me oh so close,
be kind and romantic and call me your sweet rose?

Are you the one who will catch me when I fall,
and always stand by me to confront one and all?

Are you the one who will join me as a team,
to love, honour and cherish or are you just a dream?

Tracy Ellen Jones

INSIDE THE ATTIC

Have you ever thought what goes on up here?
Corruption, deception causing a stir.
Twisted, barbaric demons at play,
Forcing and urging you every step of the way.

Alcohol fuels them, drugs do the same,
They feed off your emotions, playing this game.
Déjà vu flashback, what's going on?
Whispering and chanting, singing their song.

I tell them to stop it, the pain they inflict,
The laughter and torments, they're making me sick.
Tampered genetics, blood-curdling screams,
Is it hereditary, passed down through genes?

I look in the mirror, it's there in my eyes,
Like a wolf in sheep's clothing, a perfect disguise.
I wish I was normal, or is everyone insane?
The Lord has the answers, I believe he's to blame.

Lee Blandon

THE BIG PIT

Darkness crept around me
Lurking in the corners
Hiding in the walls
Paralysing me in its terrible glare.

Dampness swam around me
Filling the air with a foul smell
Leaping on my skin
Then trickling back off.

Dirt flew around me
Flying on invisible wings
Filling the air with a musty taste
And painting me a deadly black.

Amber Chester

WHY CAN'T MEN BE MORE LIKE US?

Why can't men do the washing, ironing and make a cup of tea,
Why has it always got to be me?
Why can't men change the bed, or clean the loo
And even clean up Baby's poo?
Why can't men cook dinner at night?
With both of us working, it would be a change all right!
And what about dental appointments and school teachers to see?
'I'm too busy, too tired,' we've heard it before,
I get so angry I should show him the door.
'I'm meeting the boys tonight,' they say,
'Would you drop me off and pick me up? I won't be late.'
It seems to me we've sealed our fate.
We do the job of two
But while we put up with it, this will carry on
Until we make a stand and even out the pace
We will always be the inferior race.

Carol

A LIFE OF CONFUSION

Walking through the shaded trees
I've been ushered down this path
But now I'm left without the keys
And can't stand the aftermath

The clouded sky hides the light
No help to find my way
So now I'm left in the night
With nothing to stop me stray

Where I stand the mist draws in
Until I am surrounded
I feel it permeate my skin
I feel I'm being hounded

Nowhere to run, no place to hide
I'm searching for my course
Impossible without a guide
Or some other mystic force

As the wind intensifies
No decision or conclusion
No escape from my demise
No chance it's just illusion

So how does this story end
How am I to find my way
I'll simply lie and pretend
And fight this another day

K Jenkins

YOU

(For my wife Fiona)

To know I'm with you today, tomorrow, forever,
is to know endless bliss.
To know such beauty surrounds me
is to know ecstasy.

Your beauty is never-ending
always astounding and forever unexplainable.
To share your life with my life
is a far higher privilege than any accolade eternally.

To share you is ethereal.
Wherever we are; whatever the date; whatever we are doing
life is unexplainable because of you.
You are magic; you are ecstasy;
you are love and passion and all I am and have is yours.
You, You, You!

Gary George-Veale

THE INAPPROPRIATE HAT - 2004

The quiet housewife stepped off the bus,
Into a world she did not often see,
Into a world she longed for every week.
And every week, she would be seen, here, in this world of people,
A town, a place, and shops for the lonely, wild, and wicked.
And here she would come, with his list, and here she would be.
The housewife enjoyed the washing and the cooking and the cleaning
and the ironing, but every week, every blasphemous week, she would
wish for this day, this day, when she would be free, and she would go
out, and she would go shopping.
For food, for clothes, for him.
And this day, when the food was heavy in the shopping bags, and the
clothes, which were not needed, in the shops, and the windows, and
their sinful eyes, looking, piercing, and this time, yes this time, she did
not ignore.
She walked down the road. The road which had always beckoned, but
today, yes today she headed not the warnings. Betrayal. And then she
walked into a shop.
The soft lighting and quiet music, the slow murmur of people as they
drifted around, leaving a path for her to follow.
She let the escalator carry her towards the hat section.
The housewife walked towards the hats.
One particular hat.
A white-woven hat, with flowers perched atop its vast rim.
And she tried on the hat, and it fit.
And she bought the hat and he said, not a thing.

Holly Cross

A BUNDLE OF DRY WOOD

I am growing old - a bundle of drying wood
Trussed with the ties of age,
With my reason for being approaching its end.
Time - once my stalwart, generous friend -
Now regrets our liaison - repents and atones
By sucking the marrow sap from my bones,
Leaving them hollow and ripe for decay.
A place of glee where the worm will play -
With the spider within my vault of clay,
Embraced in the arms of yesterday.

Once when I was the sapling child -
With my dreams and ambitions running wild,
Ramrod straight - strong and true.
At daybreak I shimmered in the morning dew
Fuelled with belief - all doubt I eschewed.
Endowed with courage - I strode life's stage
Indelibly marking each day's stark page.
The glory seeker - the maverick speaker -
A gadabout gadfly - a narcissistic gangue,
Who heeded not as the tolling bell rang.

Philip J Mee

THAT FUNNY FEELING

Enjoying ourselves on holiday, visiting places never seen before,
Sampling the new experience, wondering what lay in store.
Parking to enjoy our picnic, spreading blankets on the ground.
There were rolls, fruit, lemonade, nature breathing all around.

Resting on the warm green grass, children playing in the meadow.
A mystic voice came calling me, 'Look beneath the
mountain's shadow.'
Rising I spied in the distance, not that very far away,
A stark long-forgotten ruin, reaching out, calling me that way.

Something far back in my memory, told me don't ignore the call,
There's something to discover, from way back when you were small.
Then I saw a hazy image, old pictures, soft, faint and a little dark,
When I last saw my special friend, inside I felt a niggling, urging spark.

I scrambled over the fallen stones, tiles, the timber and the clutter,
Something pulled me to a corner, with tears in my eyes I remembered.
In 1942, an evacuee from the bombing, five years old and
scared to death,
With my gas mask case and teddy, I was sent to a farm near Swansea.

Three years I stayed, happy days, with Dai The Sheep and
my lovely Mamgu,
The farm was near a waterfall looking down on a beautiful valley.
When the time came for me to leave, it was sudden, fast and horrid,
No time for gentle warm goodbyes, just, 'Hurry, the bus is waiting!'

No time to collect my special things, children do what they are told,
No time to find my teddy, I had to leave him in the cold.
Suddenly it all came back to me in a corner an old wooden box
Back from the time of those special years, *my teddy back at last!*

Grahame Garfield Evans

SOME WAX LYRICALLY

Now some wax lyrically and even empirically
When speaking in their native tongue
Others will borrow it from some Poet Laureate
And vowels and verbs will be flung.

Some practise deviation with clever abbreviation
Abridgers embroidering the text
So musingly mosaic and poetically prosaic
They don't quite know what to say next.

Some show exhilaration at the thought of alliteration
While for others the slang is the thing
Who scrawl their entreaty with the sword of graffiti
Juggling with jingles that wring.

Others tread carefully when speaking of hyperbole
Scurrilously scribing their scripts
Quibbling with quills in the wells of ill will
And tongues making slippery trips.

Romantic pedantics in love with semantics
In similes they all speak to me
As they stutter and stammer I don't check the grammar
Cos grammar's all Greek to me.

Andy Shaw

REFLECTIONS

What odds you'll stand unparalleled
Inside Saint Peter's Gate?
What chance that you'll be canonised
When void of earthly state?
If eyes reflect the inner soul
Then you're assured a place
In God's domain, God's promised home
Where evil shows no face.
You stand alone, a man apart,
Perfection of mankind,
Epitomising all that's good
In character and mind.
Your golden hair, that flawless face,
You enigmatic smile
Make lesser mortals seem devoid
Of grace and charm and style.
Such bearing begs for passers-by
To stop, to stand, to stare,
To marvel at such elegance
And challenge if they dare.
Broad shoulders with their hint of power,
A torso lean and tanned,
Those fatal calves, those muscled arms;
How many understand?
No more to say, it's time to end
This lesson in desire.
I know that all I see is mine,
I'll fight that inner fire.

The mirror now I'll put away
And end this daily game.
Tomorrow I can play again,
Narcissus is my name.

Paul Denver

PENARTH, OUR GARDEN BY THE SEA

Many, many years ago, we fell in love with Penarth's pleasant shore.
Victorian town by the sea, lovely gardens and property.
Stately buildings in it found, and pleasant gardens by seashore's sound.
Not far from Cardiff's busy streets are we, an outing for a
                              shopping spree.
Across the channel on a summer's day, a paddle steamer makes its way.
Victorian pier proudly stands, over muddy seas and gritty sands.
On promenade folks parade, past cafés and shops their wares displayed.
Italian gardens, look continental, relaxing to music sentimental.
New large marina, a peaceful place, boats moored here, as sea
                              yachts race.
Lifeboat ever standing by, for each urgent call or cry.
Pleasant parks to wander around, shady trees flower and bird sound.
Cosmeston Lakes and village medieval, on the beach find
                              relics primeval.
On the cliff top so pleasant to roam, with views of Weston, Flat
                              and Steep Holm.
Not too far to travel the vale, or up to the valleys from whence
                              we did hail.
In Penarth's past history, the docklands outlet for coal out to sea.
Of famous people we've had quite a few, Joseph Parry,
                    Saunders Lewis, Guy Gibson resided here too.
The resort is most popular, visitors flock from near and far
But still remains so tranquil, hopefully it always will.

Eirlys Thomas

PHONEY MALONEY

Phoney Maloney the little grey pony
Had lived all his life by the sea
So Phoney Maloney the little grey pony
Was as happy as could be.

Phoney Maloney the little grey pony
Took children for rides on the beach
Until Phoney Maloney the little grey pony
Was taken and kept out of reach.

Phoney Maloney the little grey pony
Was found to be getting too old
So Phoney Maloney the little grey pony
Was taken off to be sold.

Phoney Maloney the little grey pony
Was feeling ever so sad
So Phoney Maloney the little grey pony
Decided that he would be bad.

Old Phoney Maloney the little grey pony
Had made a disguise for his ears
So Phoney Maloney the little grey pony
Escaped back down to the piers.

Phoney Maloney the little grey pony
Now wears a donkey disguise
So Phoney Maloney the little grey pony
Gives the children a great big surprise.

Rebecca Shelley

UNTITLED

In one state, I would her keep,
a delicate angel resting in sleep.
Her mind twists and turns deep,
a tear appears, but not to weep,
I squint my eyes to catch a peep.
I leave the bed though I have to creep
the fruits of labour are hers to reap,
So why next to me, does she keep?

Kieron McCullar

KYRIE

Kyrie, Kyrie, Kyrie, Kyrie, Kyrie, Kyrie
God help us, help us all to help each other,
Alleluia, Alleluia,
I love you God Alleluia
Save me for yourself
Alleluia, Alleluia
Rest my soul, rest my soul
Alleluia, Alleluia,
Keep my soul, keep my soul for Yourself
Alleluia
Amen.

R E Keane

I HEAR VOICES WEEPING

I hear voices weeping,
From deep within my skull.
Their desperate echoes wailing,
Like the screeching of a gull.

Whispers shrilly shrieking
My insanity's increasing
The noise is penetrating
My madness they're creating
They whisper when I dream
I hold my head and scream
I rock back and forth, but
Through my thoughts they cut
Piercing, screaming, sobbing, crying
I fear my mind is slowly dying
Surrounding whiteness blinds me
I know I'll never be free
They watch me through the glass
Wait until the rages pass
Chanting, wailing, hissing, howling
The voice inside my head is prowling
Now a needle in my arm
Soon they hope I will be calm
Sedatives coarse through my vein
Electric currents shock my brain
Restrictive cloth, a padded cell
Imprisoned in a stark white hell
Lying on my bed I stare
They leave the room I'm unaware
The voice inside, no longer violent
The world around is deathly silent
I do not hear their footsteps creeping.

I still hear the voices weeping

Cathryn Davies & Lynsey Davies

SAILING BY MYSELF

I'm locked up now, in a cell
Don't get out, till the breakfast bell
I hear a creak, out in the corridor
I just can't take this anymore.
Why are they outside and I am in?
So many reasons, I can't even begin.
All I know is that they're out there
While I stay put, it isn't fair.

It's like sailing by myself on a lake
Only there're chances I need to take
But out there I wouldn't have a hope to cling to
No confrontations I need to get through
But in here there is a claustrophobic space
I wish I was in another place.

I'm stuck in here on my own
No one to talk to, not even a phone.
It's just me and the walls in this heavy cell
I feel I'm stuck inside a well.

It's like sailing by myself on a lake
Only there're chances I need to take.
Either way there's only me
Inside this cell no view to see.

The point I'm trying to make
Is I'll be lonely even on a lake.
Will I ever be free?
All I need is the cell key

But whatever, I'm in prison
And the problem has arisen
I've got the old inmate's bug
No way out, the tunnel can't be dug.

David Jones (14)

MY NATURE

The wind in the sky up high in the night
And the trees on the ground rustling.
The shelter is above the ground.
The worms in the mud squiggling around.
The rabbits run by.
The footpath appears to my eye.
Underground the moles run about
And I walk by with the fire flames up high
And I read a book.
And I enjoy the views of the mountains and trees.
The streams run past.
The fire smoke gets blown up high.
The horses trot by.
The mountains go for miles.
The sound of the sea on the beach.
When I sing the sound travels through the forest.
The snowy hills and the sound of the rain.
The smell of the woodsmoke makes me happy.
In the night I hear the rustling of the animals as they go by.
The spirit inside makes me feel nature all around.
The birds in the sky sing up high.

Alex French (9)

THE SEA

Swirling, swishing, swaying, the sea.
I feel somehow it's teasing me.
Crashing, thrashing onto the beach.
It's calling to me, 'Set yourself free.'
Whispering, whirling, twirling the waves.
It's saying, 'Come and stay for the day.'
Breaking, snaking onto the shore.
It's asking me to adore it some more.
Ever-changing and lasting, that's how the sea is to me.
Untold beauty nature has provided for thee.

Beverley French

MY SON

My son's life is over, no more will I see
His handsome young face smiling down at me.
His life was so short but so full of love,
From people he worked with and those above.
From friends and relations, prisoners too,
He suddenly died, they were all so blue.
The Scrubs was a morgue, they were all quiet,
Their respect shown in the quietest riot.
I will miss him for the rest of my life,
And his death will always cut like a knife.
My love for him is a blooming flower,
That will grow and grow with every hour.
He will never look old, or bent, or ill,
But oh those hours of my life he won't fill.
And wherever he is, I hope he has joy,
Love and happiness that death can't destroy.

Nicolette Andréa Thomas

THE MAGIC OF CHRISTMAS

The magic of Christmas
It's that time of the year,
Oh! The magic of Christmas
Is having you near.

I remember that feeling
And that moment of joy
When our children were little
And the fun with their toys!

To live life without you
Is something I fear,
My life is complete now
Just having you here.

The magic of Christmas
Comes from Heaven above,
It's a time for forgiving
And to reach out your love.

Yes, the magic of Christmas
Are those you hold dear,
But the magic of Christmas
Is having you here!
Yes the magic of Christmas
Is having you here.

Molly Meehan

BUNNY LOVE

'What happened?' said the hedgehog as he wandered fairly cautiously,
across the dew-wet lawn at break of day.
'I was thrown out of a window in a temper, very bumpily,'
said Teddy from the grass on which he lay.

'Don't think this is the first time cos it isn't and I am used to it -
I like the peace and quiet by myself.
Don't worry - someone from the house will come and get me presently
and go and put me back upon the shelf.'

He lay there with one leg up in the air and murmured dreamily.
The hedgehog heard him say, 'My ears are wet,
I fear that I have lost my coat, my growl went many years ago,
but in my breast my heart beats strongly yet.

So listen to my tale of love - don't snort like that it's very rude.
This story's bound to touch your eyes with tears.
I saw her in the window with the ducklings and the Easter eggs,
- her little snow-white paws and floppy ears.

Oh Hedgehog how her ears did flop! Her black eyes shone so beadily!
Her fur it looked so soft and shiny white!
She smiled at me - I know she did - the world turned over crazily,
I looked and longed till she was out of sight.

For once he didn't throw me out. The pram went bumping on and on -
We'll never meet again. Alas! Alas!
Some horrid little girl will have her, treat her with great cruelty
and throw her out of windows on the grass.'

W Huggett

THE LOST DOOR

Where is the door that is open to all?
Was it pushed
Or did it fall?
Why do we now see clouds in a sky?
Do we need wings in order to fly,
Or is it Heaven beyond those portals,
An uplifting experience for ordinary mortals?

Rachel E Joyce

TRUTH AND JUSTICE

War, famine, world destruction, greed, pleasure how do you function?
People dying, people scared, will this world ever be prepared?
Peace, peace, we all cry peace, when will all these things cease.
Soon, soon, we hear the cry, but all we hear is many more lies.
We can't stop now we're nearly there, then this world will soon be fair.
Who do they kid, with their twisted tongues, legs crossed twiddling
their thumbs.
'We know best,' we hear them say. 'We know the better way.'
They tickle our ears, with a word and a phrase, as our world is
in a blaze.
'When will it stop?' we all do cry. It will stop when you choose I.

Charles Gonthier

WINTER

A carpet of white frosty snow,
The temperature cold and extremely low.
The trees like skeletons, reaching above,
The rooftops as white as a flying dove.

The lake turned into a mirror of ice,
Colourful decorations, looking homely and nice.
Lights of red, yellow and green,
Stars shining down like a powerful beam.

Happy songs and cheery voices,
The village alive with many noises.
A little robin, flying from tree to tree,
Many new things to hear and see.

Christmas trees looking lovely and neat,
Happy voices all over the street.
At the top of the tree, an angel with silver wings,
Dressed as beautifully as princes and kings!

Winter has come, everyone is happy,
The dog, the fish and next door's old tabby.
The stars on the trees brightly glitter,
Everybody enjoys a good snowy winter!

Rebecca Thomas

JUST DREAMING

Often have I sat on a sandy beach or in a sheltered cove.
Just dreaming.
Watching seagulls soaring high and skimming waves.
Then scavenging among the jetsam on the shore.
Just dreaming.

Feeling jealous as I watch the sea caress the sand as gently
as a lover's hand.
Just dreaming.
Sometimes at night when all alone, I sit in peace,
Watching moonbeams playing games along the crests of rolling waves.
Just dreaming.

The waves roll in and *lash* the sand, no warm embrace and
lingering stay.
Emotions change from *love* to *hate,* an angry swirl and out again.
Still all alone I sit and watch the sea and sand.
No longer dreaming.

If only I could find a niche to store away those dreams
Of loving thoughts and tenderness.
Then somehow recall in times of stress,
While in the throes of deep despair and loneliness.
Still dreaming.

Jack Jenkins

PNEUMOCONIOSIS
(Black Lung Disease)

In intricate ways,
the black dust
had mapped out his life.

In the bronchioles,
alveoli of his lungs;
seams of coal had settled.

He mined mucus now,
this small, shrivelled man
from Ynysybwl -
coughing up his guts
on cold, dark days in Wales.

Compensation took him to China,
where he met the Terracotta Army;
walked the Great Wall,
as far as he could,
on the strongest of steroids -
three inhalers to hand.

Over a bitter,
we talked.

After all;
his surgeon had said -

'Enjoy yourself.'

Marc Harris

COMING AND GOING

Each passing year about this time
We try to conjure a little rhyme
To tell our friends - whom we hold dear
The essence of our family's sphere.
A new leaf was added to the family tree
When the Blodgett household changed from two to three.
The parents know they have one of a kind
A brighter trio would be hard to find
Meg and Bron are steeped in books
Tom in the kitchen learning to cook
Maybe one day we'll see a masters degree
What is done with it now, we're eager to see
Youth is a gift of nature, old age a work of art,
They are working as artists - while we keep young at heart.
As time flies by and older we grow
The more we appreciate the friends we know
Life is a little brighter when we think of you
Don't think we're joking, it's really true.
Friends are like oxygen we breathe from air
Without either - life would be stilted - bare
May your path be strewn with flowers,
Memories, friends and happy hours,
May blessings come from Heaven above
To fill your life with peace and love.
Life is fragile - handle it with care
Love is God's gift - accept it with prayer.

Susannah Burston

RIVER OF JOY

I ask God to unblock
my river of joy.
Who first blocked
the flow of my joyous delight
from where it issued forth
like molten gold?
Joy is the heart's currency.
It bubbles and giggles
irrepressibly across boulders
placed in its way.
It is gleeful and twinkling,
playfully it skips and hops
and cartwheels to your door
bearing gifts lightly,
singing songs sweetly.
The heart is innocent and kind.
It does not trap or steal,
but only beams its approval.
Joy is warm and glowing.
It melts all resistance.
What is hard yields
and loses its grip.
It will not be extinguished
or turned away
until it has captured your smile.

Gina Fisher

OLIVER

(Or sometimes known as 'Olly')

I met this little 'fellow' - with the short fat hairy legs
Who looks at you appealingly and then sits up and begs
With such a wistful look upon his chubby face - his ears
Alert to catch the faintest sound - ah! the postman he hears
And rushes to the front door - awaiting the letters to drop
Through the letterbox they fall - and suddenly, bop!
He pounces on the pile of paper - in minutes it is shredded
Then a pair of hands on him descend - and he is promptly bedded.

I met this little 'fellow' when I called to have some lunch
With my sister (that's where he lives). So I took a bunch
Of flowers, some grapes and a chicken - ready cooked
My sister had been poorly - but now feeling better, looked
Very smart as the door she opened - little 'fellow' by her side
He wagged his tail and cocked his head - eyes open very wide
He seemed to say - oh! no - another? I hope they don't just talk
I'd really like to have some food and then go for a walk.

It wasn't long before he knew that chicken was on the table
He sniffed around then wagged his tail and if only he'd been able
He would have jumped up to help himself before it all went cold
But he's a lovely little 'fellow' - and always does what he is told.
Well nearly always - except sometimes when the door's been left ajar
He'll rush outside and run around - but never goes very far.
You just call his name out - Oliver - or sometimes just shout 'Olly'!
And back he runs - on his little legs - he makes everyone feel so jolly.

(He's a lovely little 'fellow' - and my sister thinks so too
But I haven't told Oliver that we used to call her 'Moo'.)

Pamela L Davies

THE BLACK MOUNTAINS

The cold wind blows
A frozen knife on your cheek
The grey of the sky, the green of the grass
The view is enough to make your knees weak.

The earth like a sodden sponge
The trees twisted like spent matches
The bracken grabs at our ankles and trips us up
Full of hidden traps and catches.

A little mountain pony
Brings a warm smile to our hearts
The thistles pierce our skin
Digging in like poison darts.

As we climb up a rock staircase
We eye a little cave
Scattered with bones, we realise
It must be an animal's grave.

B L Bennell (13)

BEFORE I GO

Our faces blister then burn.
The hiss of chemicals, released by heat,
Accompany silent flames.
In a metal bucket. I stare up at myself, then twist and flare

Your occasional presence is incidental.
It's me that is being eradicated tonight.
Burning all my yesterdays with you.
My very last labour, in the garden we once shared.

All other photos of you, alone or with friends,
On holiday, in clubs, bars and restaurants,
All those miscellaneous records of spent moments,
Are safe and sound, preserved.

I have rendered you a service.
For tomorrow when you and he
Make a new life together,
I shall not appear at inopportune moments.

Years from now, in reflective mood,
Looking through old albums.
Will you momentarily break, that spell of self-absorption
And wonder who it was, that held the camera.

Karl Williams

FREEDOM
(Armistice Sunday)

Although this day brings back sad mem'ries,
We can share its blessings too;
Freedom's flag is flying higher
Trumpets sound the message true;
All our hopes and aspirations
Intermingle with the past
Dispersing clouds of war and thunder,
Peace we celebrate at last;

We must not fail in this our duty,
While we serve our Lord and Crown;
May an avalanche of longing
Wipe away each worried frown;
As we stand with pride and honour
May we share a mutual trust
Keeping the torch alight for freedom
In this conflict of the just;

May we still strive with renewed vigour,
For the cause of Mother Earth;
While we pray in faith for guidance
Help us Lord to prove our worth;
All the triumphs of the ages
Part of God's eternal plan
For this dear land we love and cherish,
Perfect peace, ordained for man.

Ernest H Cottle

BLOSSOM

Watching from her window
The last snow melts as
Spring pushes its way through the cold
And out of the branches.

The world goes by without her,
It whirls.
The walls of her mind are restrictive
The loss of her mind is oppressive.

Watching from her window
The last leaves fall as
Winter spreads its bitter cold
Over the branches, but
A spring-warm voice calls
'Blossom.'

Abby O'Sullivan

BRIAN

bRian and drugs
were like pEas in a pod
the demon drink Sought our brian a lot
life was like a parTy

whIch was best enjoyed stoned
the playstatioN essential

Played best with a grudge
bragging points Earned
but always Another chance to come good
not now the sCores have become a result
brian's left the building thE game's over by default.

Christopher Bolton

UNTITLED

Over the hills and far away
Next year, in the distance, in the mist
Future, a whole new number, a fresh start
Centenary   continuing in to
Celebrations   The new millennium
Cardiff   The twenty-first century
Doctor Who   peace, hope, respect
Youth giving a voice
Equality black and white
Unity family
Religion media
Respect digital
Recycling God
Futuristic global
Bring me sunshine
Food enough, community
Care, fresh water for all
Nature, humans, wildlife
Communication dreams

Help
Darkness
Neighbourhood
Love is all you need
Security warmth
Who knows
What lies
Ahead
?

Luke Todd

ONE MORE TRY

Please my love I am asking you,
For one more try to prove it's true.
That I love you with all my heart,
To prove to you we must not part.

Happiness and joy we used to share,
When we were together and really cared.
We loved each other through thick and thin,
So why my love should we give in?

Give in to hardship and pain,
We fought it once, we can fight it again.
We planned our future to be grand.
So what went wrong? I don't understand.

So please my love, let's try again,
To build our love without any pain
With love and happiness and joy to share,
Like we once had when we were a pair.

J Bendall

PLANET EARTH

Petrol fumes, chemical leaks and oil spills
so much damage done it gives me chills.

Holes in the ozone, global warming
floods, dry seasons here's our warning.

Bickering and endless fighting
electric and neon lighting.

The world is a horrible place
made that way by the human race.

Wars waging here and everywhere
the USA and Britain, what a pair.

Have we listened, do we care?
Our lives are in the hands of Mr Blair.

Deborah Remnant

THE PHOTOCOPIER - A GUIDE

Approach with even mood and open heart
When duplicating don't depart
Or back again return to start,
Don't use haste if time is short
And racing risk renowned report
Or best laid plans it will abort.
When sure you asked for only one
A countless cascade could come
Quite a tidy little sum.

Now jamming up, ignoring pleadence
And many times to test your credence
You will have to show allegiance,
Now follow on-screen service ritual
And pray it won't become habitual
You'll have humble pie as bitter victual.
If your temper's lost just walk away
Try not to let it rue your day
'C'est la vie' you must say,

To work all day - it won't take much
Rest your hand with loving touch
And kind will be returned as such.
But please remember with this tool
Heed the warning be no fool
It's a god whose heart is cruel.
So try to learn this refrain
A peaceful mind you can gain
With vital data to maintain.

Beyond all else my dearest reader
Do not use the auto feeder!

Steve Gorvin

UNTITLED

Hands mittened by the cold
prepare soil
bony shovels create
space for a bulb.

It was long in construction
idea fragments gathered
with diamond-tipped tweezers
leaves, flakes and wings of
sun burn, wind-chap, razor-cut
stitched together with
lines from worms
murdered for purpose in
boiling water
thread unbroken so
to stretch skin sari
shaped around
a word, a memory
of a kiss or a photograph or a thought
containing nothing.

There is no envelope netted back
no picture telling of how it will look
if it blooms
no paper, no receipt, no return.

The neighbour's cat
aerates the dirt with purrs
and fertilises well
happy to be of service
to the roots' wait.

The leaves will be scarlet
thick petals
gloss arranged perfect
fibonacci with helix fractalled in
impress your face flat
on the wall of my kitchen.

I wash dishes, blow air
to make the shadows work at something different.

Annabelle Mooney

ADIEU, COLD KNAP

We'll never forget that old Cold Knap pool
Of those carefree days, days of youth and of school
That loved, oblong basin, out in the open air
For swimming, all day, was beyond all compare

My mind wanders back - back to summer, '91
And the long, hot days, on the Knap, in the sun
Around that large bath, did we all pose around
Jealously guarding our small patch of ground
'Twas our own Venice Lido, here in Barry, South Wales
For swimming, and tanning, and eyeing females!
Fathers and sons, along with mothers and daughters
All came to the Knap, with its icy cold waters
The water was freezing, sure, that much was true
Out you would come, frozen solid and blue
You'd towel yourself dry, and feel right as rain
And then take the plunge, for five lengths once again
When you felt brave, you would dive off top boards
Fearing you'd 'belly flop' in front of the hoards
For leisurely backstroke, on your back you would lie
Keeping your form, looking up at the sky
Racing your pals, over widths and long lengths
When the day was over, you were happy, but spent
You'd breaststroked and crawled and tried butterfly strokes
And picnicked together, with laughs and with jokes.

And now that old pool is not there any longer
And absence sure does, make the heart grow much fonder
A council decision - some suited man's whim
Has taken our pleasure, and filled our pool in
Those long summer days now will never come back
For gone is the pool, by the sea, on the Knap
Those halcyon days are left far behind
But those summers, in Barry, how they stick in the mind.

Timothy Cross

NEW JERSEY GIRL

I once knew a girl from the New Jersey shore
Who was so beautiful she entered folklore.
Towns like Seaside Heights, Belmar, Avon By The Sea
She's a girl who means everything to me.

All New Jersey is known for is garbage dumps and heavy industry,
People don't know about the miles and miles of
                              beautiful land by the sea.
Ellis Island and The Statue of Liberty are both in New Jersey waters,
And I fell in love with one of its daughters.

Jenny O'Connell was her name
Since I met her my life has never been the same.
For she will always own my heart,
Just like she has from the start.

During the War of Independence New Jersey was
                              right in the thick of things
For the American nation was rebelling against the British king.
And even though I can't be with her a lot of the time,
To her with love I dedicate this rhyme.

A J Heyward

REAL LOVE

What is love? It is a dream,
It takes you up and it brings you down
And on a Merry-go-round.
It is full of light, that goes off and on,
But hold on tight, before it has gone.
Hold one another when you can,
Say 'I love you' every day
And don't stray away.
Real love comes once in a lifetime,
So don't throw it away,
It won't come back just like another day.

Beryl Elizabeth Moore

FACTORY CHRISTMAS

The fifty something loaded bra,
Pointing at the boys.

The quiet IT man,
Strutting John Travolta.

The pinstripe nosing,
Halves of bitter with the boss.

The cellophane dress from packing,
Remembering Friday,
Scared to death on Sunday . . .

David R Thompson

ABERFAN

The little town of Aberfan has left a tragic mark,
That grim October morning, the weather bleak and dark,
The rain came down in torrents, the wind was blowing wild,
As children walked towards their school, the children meek and mild.
Excited, and so happy of the day that lay ahead,
Their little satchels on their backs, their blazers grey and red.
At nine o'clock that tragic morn, there was a mighty roar,
Men knew it wasn't thunder, as they rushed towards the door.
They feared the worst would happen, that grim and darkened day,
And sensed a coal tip sliding, they were numb in every way.
Those black and ugly monsters that reached towards the sky,
An erupting black volcano as the wind and rain lashed by.
The coal tip was so angry, like a wild demented giant,
And started sliding down the hill, so black, so cold, defiant.
Gushing, swirling, rushing, the blackened mud rushed through,
Everyone was helpless, there was nothing one could do.
Thick and blackened slurry came rushing down the slope,
A farmhouse was demolished - could there be any hope?
Children now were screaming as they saw the blackened slurry,
Engulfing all their village school, there was no time to hurry.

Children they were buried 'neath stone and ugly coals,
Rescuers were fighting hard to reach these poor souls.
Panic now engulfed the scene, with men and women crying,
Digging on relentlessly, they did not give up trying.
The rain still came in torrents, the winds so very strong,
Searchers came from everywhere, they laboured all night long.
Some children they were rescued, still screaming for their mates,
Why did this have to happen - why was it their school gates?
Many children's lives were claimed beneath the gruesome rock,
Devastated families were filled with pain and shock.
As long as I shall live on Earth, I can't forget this day,
A children's generation was so sadly snatched away.
The landscape now is verdant, where giant coal tips lay,
Though landscaped and much greener, the memories they will stay.

That day of devastation, so cruel, full of hate,
Why our little children - why did they meet their fate?
There'll never be an answer, as we look toward the sky,
And people all around the world still ask the question *'why?'*
They'll never be forgotten, and life will carry on,
We'll always see them smiling, in Wales their land of song.

Marjorie J Picton

MOUNTAINS

The mountains I see from my window
Change their appearance from day to day.
Today is rather misty they look dismal and grey.
Yesterday the sun shone, they were sparkling green,
Tomorrow could be raining, then cannot be seen.
In winter, snow sits like icing on a cake,
In spring see lambs jumping each morning when I wake.
Summer brings the lovers, strolling arm in arm,
Halfway up the mountain, they rest at a farm.
Autumn is much cooler, wimberry pickers appear,
There's a lot of fruit to gather at this time of year.
I love to look at the mountains, see the changes taking place,
Every day a different picture, every day a different face.

J P Williams

THE GIRL ON CILGWYN MOUNTAIN

We met in a sun filtered drizzle long ago, long ago
Her hair was black as midnight and eyes of moss green.
The lingering sunlight gave the drizzle a greenish hue
And we were for a while, lost in this turquoise tranquillity
On the slopes of 'Cilgwyn Mountain'
In the gradually diminishing light, almost sixty years ago.

She was so beautiful, but oh! so very young, barely thirteen
Was she, and fifteen was I, and soon off to sea,
But we were to meet many times in the years to come.
When departing Liverpool through the Irish Sea for distant venues
I always gazed at my homeland, and remembered the girl on Cilgwyn
Mountain, with hair as black as midnight, and eyes of moss green.

After six years or so, I left the sea forever
I still remember the heaving decks in storms extreme
The moonlit quietness of the wheelhouse at night
And the sea of dark blue glass.
Once again I started seeing the girl on Cilgwyn Mountain
With hair as black as midnight and eyes of moss green.

I started driving my father's tipper lorries throughout Wales
And was now regularly courting my girl on Cilgwyn Mountain.
We were married one cold November morn in the aftermath of a storm
We were so much in love, me and my girl on Cilgwyn Mountain
With hair as black as midnight and eyes of moss green.

Now we are retired and daily growing older,
We reside in Fron village at the foot of Cilgwyn Mountain
We still walk the mountain slopes, often in gentle drizzle
I still dearly love my girl on Cilgwyn Mountain, with silver hair
Like spring moonlight, and still eyes of moss green!

Wyn Williams

MEN HAVE ALWAYS LOVED ME BUT I'M NO WOMAN!

There are these singular and unique places,
they bring a smile to all men's faces.
Brick built, some signless, some bright shiny red,
these are places to which I've sped.
These wee small buildings have no roof,
so hardly are they waterproof!
And not a place for ladies these,
but where men themselves they seize!
So many have to these made haste,
the only reason can be for waste.
How many times as boy then man,
have gentlemen used them when they can.
When desperate they wander from the pub,
or staggering homeward from the club.
Or just caught short as they drive by,
these places only for a guy.
So here it is that waters flow,
copiously from standers in a row,
but understand never for no. 2's,
these often old but well used loos!

Huw D Jones

AN OLD CHURCH

Built in a field so far away
Abandoned and so cold,
A church standing all alone
Walls tall, erect and bold.

Graves that do encircle are
Proof of all those that came,
To this Holy Sanctuary
To praise and sing His name.

Both wooden doors are now shut
All people have now gone,
Silence felt within its walls
And singing there is none.

Clifford Jones (Meirion Fab)

LUMINESCENT HUES

Luminescent hues
Shimmer,
As a multicoloured arc
Thrusts high,
In misty rain.

Outstretched,
To grasp mocking sunbeams,
As black horses
Of clouds prance
Across the sky.

Polly Davies

SWEET WELSH MOUNTAINS

The sweet Welsh mountains
Of my home
I see them every day
They loom outside my window
Like gods who rule the day

When I'm away I miss them
Like friends I've left at home
But I'll always come back home to them
No matter where I roam

So green and free in summertime
They call to me each day
But white with snow in winter
Stay away they seem to say

When my time is up
They'll lay me there
Beneath them hills of home
I'll lie beneath my mountains
And no more will I roam.

D T Baker

DUST

The sunlight lights the dance
That gives a second glance
Of dust and pollen floating
And bombarding you by chance
These millions of unseen particles
That live in the ether above
Can only be seen in sunlight
And increase at the pat of a glove
You may look into a rock pool
Or on the earth below
But in the air
Millions are there
And gone with the wind's first blow!

Ron Houghton

THE CELTIC FRINGE

Breathing Wales see the
Reborn Dylan Thomases
In a myriad differing forms.

Hear with hollow ears
Oft repeated words
Six days of the seven.

Prophets of the dells reclaimed
Singing with wild locks
And shiny suits.

Are convulsed with the agony
Of exile . . . be it only
A league across the border.

And what then of the sheep?
The feckless, rugged, travelling
Mountain sheep.

Pursued across the patchwork hills
By a million poets with
Anthem-echoed themes.

Who dwell in Cymru may
Long-love the lambs
But nightly dwell with dragons.

Sarah Blackmore

LITTLE STAR SHINING BRIGHT

Little star shining bright,
Shine on me, give me light,
Through this darkness I can't see,
Little star shine down on me.

When God sent Jesus down to Earth
He sent a star to guide His birth,
In a stable dark at night,
You were there to shine your light.

While shepherds left their flocks in fright,
And followed oh that star so bright,
Three wise men came from afar,
Guided by that shining star.

Little star shine down on me,
And guide me to where I can see.
To a world without no strife,
Where we can live a better life.

With people living side by side,
No colour, creed, or race denied,
Without no wars, just peace on end,
Little star you'll be my friend.

May Rigby

DISILLUSIONMENT

Jessie has gone to London Town
To study for a law degree
And now the paths through Ilston Woods
Are only for the birds and me.

All summer long we'd ramble free
Loving each other's company
And delighting in each glorious hour
Through this wonderland of Gower

From Oxwich Marsh where the herons stand
To Horton Beach with its golden sand
From Fairy Hill to Overton Mere
And Paviland Cliffs where the sea runs clear

Past Burry Green where the king-cups grew
To the endless wall of grey Cilfrew
And Pwll Du Head and Rhosili Down
It's a long, long way from your wig and gown

But remember this land so quiet and green
Where I was a prince, but you were a queen
When limestone rocks made a lofty throne
As we dived for doubloons off Burry Holm

Our dream was of a future fine
Along primrose paths in the bright sunshine
'We'll certainly marry some day' we'd say
But then the law got in the way

In your new life with the legal folk
Think of a boy whose heart once broke
But it's mending now, so 'good luck' from me
And I hope you enjoy your double ell bee!

Hugh Edwards

Time Capsule

The sky clear and blue a blackbird sang and
The mayor's chain glistened in the morning sun,
The capsule lowered into the brown earth,
As solemn as a funeral.
All the memories of a bygone age
Hidden for a hundred years.
Pious platitudes of a dignitary,
Seeming to go over my head,
For my inward eye saw only the shawl of blackness
That once covered the valleys.
The colliery wheels forever turning,
And pouring forth teems of work-weary miners,
Gulping fresh air into lungs hardened with coal dust.
And amidst it all the sound of laughter,
Song, poetry and philosophy.
And here in the sunshine, and solemn occasion
I feel the presence of old miners,
And I know only the things that time has forgotten,
The sorrows of widows, and blackness of memories
Collect in my thoughts, I watched the earth fall
On a million memories, and the greyness of the past
Fade into the mist of time.
I am lost now in a valley so green,
The greenness a kind of sadness
That covers the earth's scars and grief,
In the warmth of a summer's day,
Amidst the green hills of Rhondda
Ghosts of old miners hovered
And the blackbird sang a dirge.

Phyllis Bowen

FACTORIES ON THE WIRRAL

Teenage like they sprawl
Unsightly across the land.
Their spewing chimneys
Puff out poisons to the air,
Like careless cigarette ends.

Stephen Parry

HEAVEN'S NEW ANGEL

We visit her home for the final time,
Dressed in black with tears a plenty,
The windows are damp, and the door is wide,
The house is full, but her chair is empty.

The wreaths line the stairs, like the steps to Heaven,
My immortal gran asleep in her box,
And this is just God's fateful warning,
That there's nowhere to hide when the Reaper knocks.

We parade her beneath the mourning sky,
The coffin heavy, from the weight of her salvation,
Because this time last week Granny got saved,
But today doesn't feel like a celebration.

The church aisles are rivers of sadness,
And the family falls in, just like the eventide,
We're swept away in a current of emotion,
But this is not the end, this is just goodbye.

Sniffling in the graveyard, crying church chimes,
The coffin is light in the absence of sin,
Walking in time to constant whimpers,
Death will come but never win.

All heads are bowed surrounding the burial,
Still tears left, though only just,
Heaven opens up as Granny descends
. . . Ashes to ashes, dust to dust.

So Nana is gone, but not forgotten,
If it wasn't for her none of us would be,
Living out moments of happiness,
And days of uncertainty.

Ian McNamara

COWS NEED LUXURIES!

The countryside is covered,
Most of it with cows.
The grass must feel smothered,
Under all those cows.

All fields have dark patches,
Usually with mud or poo.
All those lazy cows,
Why can't they use the loo!

I suppose it doesn't help
If we don't give them a hand,
Make toilet bowls much bigger,
So on their bums they won't land.

Cows also need some luxuries,
How about a bath?
Then all the cows will smell nice
A hot tub! Then they can have a laugh!

Or maybe cows are happy just the way they are,
Maybe they would like tea and sugar
Or try out clothes and beds,
Oh who cares, I am eating a beef burger!

Philippa Jayne Sterritt (13)

READING MY THOUGHTS

If you read my poetry, then you're reading my thoughts
About the beautiful scenery or the Creator we've got
I'm expressing my feelings, my sorrow, or love
My escapes, my relationships, and thoughts from my heart
A release from emotions or from moments of care
And some precious thoughts with others I've shared
The poems I've written have been a solace to me
When I've opened my heart and my feelings ran free
I'm so many places and so many lands
On London's streets, America, Africa and Ireland.
On park benches, and prisons, lonely people and friends
Just to mention strange places my poems have gone
With all this in mind and the friends I have gained
If I write from the heart I cannot go wrong.

James McIlhatton

FROM BOY TO MAN

Sent by air, by land and sea,
To do or die, was their command.
To protect the realm, and for liberty,
Such a price to pay, for this fair land!

From boy to man, so quickly honed
Yet! Mother's children every one,
Soon, hardened fighters, nerves in tone,
Facing a foe with knife and gun.

Days and nights rolled into one!
From the hint of dawn to the sinking sun,
Hoping, praying for an end to come,
Endless battles, some lost, some won!

But now the final bugle call,
The heavy sky has turned to blue!
They gave their life, they gave their all,
So tomorrow may dawn, for me and you!

The ultimate sacrifice they made,
They've marched along their final road,
Now resting in yon stilly shades,
Where peace surrounds their last abode.

Isaac Smith

DRIVING

I'm driving down the motorway,
On this lovely autumn day,
Going to Belfast city,
To my lectures in Queen's University,

I get there just in time,
But a parking space I cannot find,
Round and round the streets I go,
Watching the students going to and fro,

In the mirror I see a parking space,
I'll park in there, now I must race,
To my lectures I must go,
To listen, learn and watch the video show,

That's all my lectures for today,
So I'll be on my way,
Back up the motorway,
And get ready for another day.

Esther Herron

FATHER AND CHILD

At Edward Hopper in *Tate* Modern,
beside vacant *Early Sunday Morning*
a tiny red-sleeved arm floats in mid air,
one small dark hand falls lightly open,
her tender palm and pristine fingers
at centre of Room 6 define perfection,
across his hip her soft calf ends in
white-socked ankle, trim black patent shoe
and when he turns, her head's nestling his chest.
Child, the man who ferries you
at three years old is sure-footed, engrossed
in colours of a dream. When he moves off
to view ocean light on sun-blown grass
of *Hills, South Truro*, my palm would trace
the steep cleft between his shoulder blades
to know such ease.

Amid crowds swarming
pictures of luminous isolation,
blind to the river in the window
and the crescent spanning the flow,
you and he stand for art and peace.

Catherine Phil MacCarthy

THE SEASONS

Shrivelled leaves laying everywhere
Trees stand still, naked and bare
Blue skies a memory of a time just passed
As autumn approaches but not to last.

Raindrops fall and turn to ice
Heating bills rise at twice the price
Hats, gloves and scarves are worn by all
Frosty layers covering the top of a wall.

Temperatures dropping all of the time
Winter approaches and is next in line
The days seem long as it always seems night
Turn the clocks back make darkness go light.

A small fall of snow fills children with glee
The first flowers of spring to make your heart happy
Daffodils, tulips and fields of bluebells
Fill the air with warmth and wonderful smells.

Trees redress with new coats of leaves
Honey filled flowers covered by bees
Grass to be cut, trimmed so neat
As summer approaches along with the heat.

Geoffrey Graham

MY MUM

My mother's love is always there
From her first pregnant flutter,
To her silver-grey hair,
I've always hoped that I could be
The kind of mother, that mine is to me!

J Hagen

THE JOURNEY

Waiting for my bus to come,
There's nothing left, my journey's done.

I've lived, I've loved, I've laughed, I've cried,
The lust for life inside me died.
But no regrets inside me lie,
Although I know the end is nigh.
I never lived my life in haste,
And all these years I did not waste.
Though those around me curse and weep,
The promise I made I must keep.
I shall not live another day,
And let my spirit fade away.

Waiting for my bus to come,
There's nothing left, my journey's done.

Claire Kimber (17)

GREED

The rich man accounts the cost of his yield
Harvest now complete with that last field
Ready to count his money at the table
While his neighbouring farmer is barely able

Working so hard as he labours and toils
Getting fields ready and turning the soil
No big machines on his small farm
Just a horse to help when it's cold or warm.

But surely what has the rich man got
Abundance in crops though happiness not
Whereas the poor farmer with his family of eight
Is met by them all as he opens the gate.

Though riches are something we always long
But money isn't everything, it can cause wrong
While those that have it seem to want more
Forgetting about the needy and the open door.

The poor man shares what he has on his table
With a welcome for all when he is able
Taking time to chat to a neighbour or friend
About things that matter right to the end.

For those riches and money schemes we make
Will make no difference for we cannot take
And how often we are told and heard it said
With no pockets in shrouds it's no use when dead.

Imelda Fitzsimons

I SAW JOHNNY YESTERDAY

I saw Johnny yesterday,
They say, he's been away,
I thought that he'd be special,
Recalling what they'd say.

He, the teacher's special pet,
Had hated him in school.
Clever, smart and trendy,
He had made me feel a fool.

They said, he'd make a difference,
Would shine in any test.
So why did I see Johnny
And he, looking such a mess?

His clothes were crushed and scruffy,
His eyes were wild and red.
So, smiling for a moment,
I recalled the things they said.

Had to tell the others
Just how the star turned out,
Got busy phoning all my friends,
His fall from grace to shout.

I saw Johnny yesterday,
On a talk show on TV
He asked for something special,
From people, just like me.

He wanted funds for victims
Of the famine in Sudan.
For he had come to beg for aid,
In his cushioned, wealthy land.

His dreadlocks dark and dancing,
His coloured cobra chest,
He spoke with fire and passion.
Yes! Johnny, was the best.

Mary Buckley-Clarke

SPARROWS

Sunlight is broken like rain on my window,
I wake to the sound of the light.
My eyes slowly open, like stones in the water
that washes across the dark night.

The sky's full of sparrows, and dust from the morning
that rests where the sky meets the sea.
As I stare at the eyes of the saltwater shadows
I'm trapped in the cage of the free.

And blood falls like honey across the black mirror
as ink seeps through every blank page.
The sparrows are falling, the sparrows are burning,
the sparrows are dying in rage.

They flew to the sun, to be bright, to be one,
and to blaze through the ages like smoke.
But their pillar of fire led them down to the stone
to be offered like pigeons, and choke.

The wings that were clipped are gathered together
by poets who write it all down
and pile up their paper like bodies in winter,
then scatter their ash on the ground.

But blackbirds are perched on the tree of our lives
as worms eat the apple of words.
The beautiful sunset that hoists on the branches
is melting like gold on the birds.

The the sparrows were singers, and liars, and killers,
on trial by all that they made.
Their feathers were trodden, and trembled, unfinished,
in terror of being afraid.

We could not write the beginning or ending
but we must sail somewhere between,
and hide like the partisans cloaked in a sandstorm,
and die like the sparrows unseen.

David Russell

MY LOVE

Many times I've told you I love you
But somehow it just isn't enough
There are no words to explain all I'm feeling
And I know it's so much more than love

These emotions take me to new places
And teach me things I never knew
It's like I'm walking on air, out of reach
I found a secret without having a clue

In a time when the world faces pain
And the tears flow steady from their eyes
I feel touched by your presence around me
And protected from the pain and the lies

This miracle that you brought to my world
Is a measure of the love that we share
For the rest of my life, good times and bad
When you need me I'll always be there

Now we face the future, much stronger
Safe in our love, because we know
This love has no boundaries or limits
And with time it continues to grow

So for taking all of those I love you's
For making them more than I've ever dreamed of
For being the best I could ever have wished for
Thank you, I love you, my love.

Linda McGrath

THE QUEEN'S BRIDGE (BELFAST)

Once old and grey and dirty
Worn out by feet - thousands
Crossed every day to work
At the 'yard' where ships were built

Machinists, welders, plumbers
Dungarees and lunch box full
Steel toe-capped boots - thousands
Polished the stone beneath their feet

Titanic, Canberra ships of fame
Born in the 'yard' fathered by men
Who crossed the bridge
Day in and day out

The 'yard's' no more
Goliath looks down on empty slipways
Grass grows where sparks flew
The bridge, lonely, looking on.

Now reborn with paint afresh
With lights of blue and stone renewed
Soft shoes, no boots to shine its stone
Its reflection proud in the river below

It's now the way to an arena of fun
The crane looks down on the people below
Ice hockey, music and fun for all
The crowds now come - thousands

They cross the bridge without a care
Don't see the shadows standing there
With boots of steel and lunch box full
Waiting for a ship to build.

John A Rea

A FARMER'S SPRINGTIME

When looking out the window on a cold December day
I thought ahead to springtime, it seems so very far away
In spring, life on the farm takes on a whole new pace
From the quietness of winter, it becomes a frantic race
The cows in their winter sheds are nearing calving time
The sheep all out in the fields have lambing on their minds
The mares in the stables are longing to be free
But with foaling time upon them this just cannot be

When people look into the fields and see new lambs at play
They don't realise the work it takes to get the lambs that way
Once lambing starts until it ends the farmer's work will double
He works non-stop to save young lambs
And help ewes who are in trouble
He eats his meals all in a rush, his hours of sleep are few
There never seems quite time enough for the work he has to do
The farmer's wife is always there at this busy time
Helping him with the sheep and with jobs of every kind
She feeds the lambs with bottles to help keep them alive
Until they are fit and strong enough
To go with their mums outside
The cold, hard earth is softening and the fields are turning green
The daffodils and snowdrops are a lovely sight when seen
In the morning we awaken to the singing of the birds
As they go about their nest building and the gathering of worms
The fields all need fertilising, some fences will need mending
For the farmer in the springtime his work is never-ending
But even at its busiest I greet each spring with cheer
It always was and will always be my favourite time of year.

Noeleen O'Neill

LITTLE ANGEL EYES

Little angels dance,
In your eyes' reflection.

And little angels prance
With love and affection.

I can see so much
In your eyes
When you're angry, hurt and despise.

If only you knew,
What these little angel eyes reveal,
Who you are,
And what you feel.

Conor McGreevy

Double Jeopardy

Blind to the unflattering selfishness of their fear,
your undeserving back has been broken by smug laughter.
Their gratitude is foolish, ignorant ungratefulness.
Yet you smile falsely at their obvious sarcasm.
Is it the mother who mixes milk with poison,
or the hungry child that drinks it,
to blame for this inequitable situation?

Anuiska Scanlon

THE LILY

So beautiful and graceful
You are by far the best
Your perfume is the sweetest
You outshine all the rest

Your petals are the palest cream
So soft and lovely, like a dream
Your velvet beauty yet untold
And in your heart pure specks of gold

Your slender body softest green
Who are you?
You're the floral queen
You are truly magnifique
No other flower can quite compete.

Maria Murray

GIANT'S CAUSEWAY

It's a picturesque scene.
All shapes of stones that gleam.

Rising to ninety metres in height
This is a wonderful sight.

There's a bus tour a day
Around the coastline to Whitepark Bay.

The legend of Finn MacCool
Causeway Girona shipwreck jewel.

Stepping he threw, if this is true?

From Causeway to Scotland
Across the seashore.
This must have been a chore.
All your famous stones named.
That gave Causeway its fame.

The Camel, The Granny, Chimney Tops, Wishing Chair,
A wish on this seems fair
The Organ, Giant's Boot
That fits his foot.

Portoon Cave travel to by sea,
Stone of key.
Honeycomb, Lordantrim Parlour,
King Of His Nobles, Punchbowl.
The Fan, they all seem grand.

Marie Coyles

THE QUEEN OF CULMORE

(In memory of a lady I once loved, written by the River Bann near Culmore in 1974)

On a farm close by, to the River Bann
Where the pines grow tall by the score
Lived a lady of beauty, whose name I'll withhold
So I'll call her 'The Queen of Culmore'.

On that farm I slaved, from dawn to dusk
Till the body grew numb and sore
But each morning I'd start, with joy in my heart,
To be near, 'The Queen of Culmore'.

On Sunday morning I took a stroll,
Along the nice river shore, on the rock in the pines.
Where the sun still shines
Sat the beautiful 'Queen of Culmore'.

Together alone, in silence we stood
God had answered my prayer once more.
In the morning mist, I sweetly kissed,
The redhead 'Queen of Culmore'.

Week after week, our love grew deep
And I promised forever more,
But others were clever, and swore
I never would marry 'The Queen of Culmore'.

'Twas nature cruel, or did I misjudge,
My friends as never before,
Then they took her from me, sent her over the sea,
My true love, 'The Queen of Culmore'.

Some years later, to Rasharkin she came,
But not to the river shore,
In the chapel they assembled, and called him a gentleman,
When he married, 'The Queen of Culmore'.

Bertie Irvine

WAITING

I'm sitting in the rain
Waiting for the train

Watching others pass
Mine is always last

I sit on my own
Wishing I was home

I hear something coming
It's the train's engine humming

I get on the train
Out of the rain

I'm into the heat
On a lovely comfy seat

Now I'm on the train
My journey starts again.

Lyndsey Herron

EMOTIONS

The human mind is so diverse, and so deceiving,
we mortals are fooled - into memories distorted,
yet go on believing.
Till all's too late, we've lost control,
and the complex mind - has claimed our soul.

Then sorrow swoops, like a wounded dove,
losing all sight of hope, of love.
To end in darkness, dank, deep in despair,
to end in silence, causing not a single stare.

All our feelings, those hypersensitive emotions,
lost from control, like the great eagle on high - soaring!
Then fast descends, through storms of rage,
leaving us sour - disenchanted - alone through ages.

Gary J Finlay

PEACE

What is peace?
Is it more than just an absence of war?
Or is it a calm deep down in the soul?

Give my head peace is a common saying.
But isn't real peace more than just an absence of noise?

Sometimes peace of the soul is hard to achieve.
Sometimes I think we an only be at peace
When we realise we are truly loved and accepted
And we learn to love ourselves.

I feel that true peace will only come in this land
When people have learned to be at peace with themselves.
True peace is internal before it reaches out and spreads.

Joanne Campbell

JIMMY'S CHRISTMAS

It's 5am and Jimmy's awake,
He picks up the stocking and gives it a shake.
Then opens the top, and has a quick look,
And pulls out some crayons and a colouring book,
A little red car, and a spinning top,
A tin of paints like the ones in the shop.

He opened his mouth and popped in a sweet,
Then groped and grappled right down in the feet,
To find an apple, orange and pear,
Hands down in further - but no more was there.
Stocking now empty, everyone else is awake,
His mother downstairs, with the breakfast to make.

He goes into the room where the big Christmas tree
Stands in the corner where all can see.
With presents around it - some big and some small,
Some are flat, but *one* is quite tall.
A photo frame for his mum and dad,
From Jimmy - their own little lad.

Christine M Tracey

CHRISTMAS CRUSH

Christmas comes once a year,
Joy and laughter, full of cheer,
Expectations running high
Wondering what to buy.

Pushing and shoving through the crowd,
You can hear the children shouting loud,
I want this, I want that,
Barbie dolls and Postman Pat.

Fairy lights and Christmas trees,
The poor shoppers feel the squeeze,
In their pocket, in their purse,
Only just started, it gets worse.

Stress levels rising, people sweat,
What can I buy the family pet?
Leave no one out at your peril,
Not forgetting Auntie Beryl.

Swollen ankles, blistered feet,
Oh my goodness! I forgot the meat,
Almost done, nearly there,
Shall I get something for Tony Blair?
Better not I'm almost skint,
I wish I had shares in the Royal Mint.

Willard Griffiths

NOT A DOG'S LIFE

Sitting in the middle of the three
I'm the smallest, can't you see?
The other two are black, white and tall
Truth be told, I'm the greatest of them all.

My ruffled feathers, my sharpened beak
They can only bark but *I can speak!*
They may walk, run and play
I can do all three but can they fly up, up and away?

They should be jealous and envy me
As I have no paws but feet like fists
I don't give sloppy's but a delicate kiss
I do not drool or slobber
As you've guessed it, I'm more graceful and proper.

I must be blunt and more direct
I am more wise, I have some intellect
I don't go around chasing my tail
The reason being it would hurt like hell.

The only problem that I seem to have
Is when people come for tea
They never seem to notice me.

Margaret Anne Morgan

TICK TICK TOCK

Tick tick tock,
Goes the grandfather clock,
It's nearly time,
To eat some lime.

Tick tick tock,
Goes the grandfather clock,
My stomach can't wait,
Until it's lunch time.

Tick tick tock,
Goes the grandfather clock,
There's some food on the table,
Yummy, it's mine!

Tick tick tock,
Goes the grandfather clock,
The food on the table
Will be gone in no time!

Emma Ritchie (11)

I AM A SNOWFLAKE

Swooping as the dark, dark night falls,
I tingle ahead of the others.
I whoosh past Aberdeen
As I run into Dundee.

I am the best circler
And fastest cool
In the ever-living
Snowflake school.

Lewis Brock (7)

GOING'S ROUGH

How could I leave you, anywhere,
I've not that many friends,
They'd take one mighty look at you,
Saying, nosey he is too,
Just there, the friendship ends,
I find it hard enough making friends,
Don't ever need your help,
You'd just but yap, and groan all day,
As like a two stone yelp,
Did you ever come to decide, in fact,
To have, a look at yourself,
There are surely few, but others,
One look at you, they're off, into the blue,
To get away, far, from your bothers,
What state was I in, you came, from within,
Saying, Mother, I am here,
Oh no, said High, it can't be a lie,
It's surely for me, coming drear,
I have to listen, to him all day,
And into the next, as well,
When asked about if I had wit, I'd shout,
And a sorry tale, I would tell,
But it's too late, for now, a change,
I'll have to put up, with you,
Please don't give me any hardships,
I'd sooner have the flu.
At least with the flu,
One can rest up, in bed,
But I take one look at you,
And my life's in a dread.

Hugh Campbell

IN THIS LIFE . . .

I watch the rain slip down the glass
Nursery's where I used to play
The sun will shine again soon
Hannah chats to Kelly
I race off to find Amanda
Smiling, we laugh our heads off,
As a passing kid becomes a boyfriend,
Dead Uncle John from Jamaica
(At least, we think he's dead . . .)
Or a dad
Lively kids run by
I chuckle at a joke Amanda's told
Fooling around, Amanda laughs
As I tell her I saw someone
With a Destiny's Child poster
Everyone's going home and I think,
'I wonder what's beyond this life . . . ?'

Melanie McLean

MUM'S A POET

Mum's a poet
And boy does she show it
Her words grace lots of books
'Here's another one dear'
Her anthem's so clear
Open it up, have a look
She's penned one on dogs
But not one on frogs
And the cats really are the cream
The words flow so well
It could make one's head swell
If you can see what I mean
Her jumble sale jargon was really a paragon
Of words thrown together with wit
I read them with pride
As she sits by my side
And realise she's not such a twit
She's got a computer
A laptop no less
I feel mass production on the cards
I will have to be patient
Just wait and see in anticipation
What's coming next from 'The Bard'.

Rosina Willox

SPIDER IN THE BATH
(Inspired by Mike Oldfield's 'Shadow on the Wall')

Spider in the bath
Spider in the bath

What is one to do?
What is one to do?

No I'm not afraid
No I'm not afraid

Go and get a glass
Put it out to grass

It won't stay in -
I am too hasty

It's really quite tiny
And no way nasty;

Oops!
Eight becomes six
(Back legs gone!)

Will she survive?
(At least she's *alive!*)

Geraint Jenkins

MY MOTHER

I have wrote so many poems but none about my mum
Many years since she passed on to somewhere up above
Oh yes, a very cheery person, yet very strict at times
I never dared to answer back, I had to toe the line
On looking back it made good sense why all the discipline
I must have been a handful: and no winged cherubim
A trifle wild and full of fun, I hated life in school
But Mum drummed it into me, not to break the rules
Said, 'Must be law and order to make our life run smooth'
Kept us clean and tidy and gave us household chores to do
Now no one should be lazy, one of her many sayings too!
Good taste too in what she wore, I was proud to call her Mum
Her clothes were never gaudy and never over done
I had to go to Sunday school, about Jesus I was taught
How he did his miracles and helps us when we're fraught
All in all she was right, so I thank her for her care and love
And hope once more to meet her when it's my turn for above.

J Prentice

MIRACLE CHILD

Into this world you came with a scream
You didn't realise you were my dream
Against all the odds you came my way
As day after day I'd sit and pray
It didn't matter if you were a girl or boy
As I knew you would fill me with bundles of joy
Watching you grow and as you play
Brings me great pleasure every day
Your mother she made, my dream come true
By giving birth to a loving son like you
Intense emotion you made me feel
Still can't believe that it's for real.
I've savoured every moment, so far that we've had
I know that I'm lucky you are my lad
I'll love and protect, give guidance too
With the hope that it helps in all that you do
You've been a little rascal at times in the past
But I knew it was a phase and wouldn't last
My miracle child that's what you are
Do as you're told and never stray far
Don't speak to strangers, run if you need
It pays to listen and to take heed.

Steven Wilson

DAISY CHAIN

This half remembered feeling:
The memory of a day
The touch of sunlight on my cheek
The butterflies at play.

The sound of distant traffic
The smell of earth and grass
The nonchalance of childhood
Whatever came to pass.

And then the clouds rolled over
And lightning lit the sky
Heavy raindrops on my head
I heard an urgent cry.

'Hurry home before you're soaked.
Run to escape the rain!'
And then the sudden panic
'I've forgot my daisy chain!'

Maureen Thomas

WARRIOR WOMEN

Warrior women, bows in hand.
Warrior women, axe to grind.
Warrior women, screeching command.
Hunting *and* gathering, sustenance to find.
Protection bearing.
Enemies scaring.
Defences wearing.
Their own hearts tearing.
Warrior women march to the fore.
Warrior women taking the strain.
Warrior women concealing their sore.
Silently nursing their dark, silent pain.

Nancy Black

ODE TO RONNIE

Ronnie what can I say, this certainly is your big day
You'll not trust anyone anymore
Leading you by the nose to Malcolm's door
The plan was hatched by many minds to take a foursome out to dine
Ronnie washed and shaved himself while Myrttle set out her best delf

No better man can we praise than Ronnie on his 65th birthday
He's always willing to help you out, no matter what the hubble's about
If it's duck eggs or dogs, cows calving, tractor in the bog
Just contact Ronnie, aye he'll be there,
Driving his Land Rover with special care

A small holding he does own, up on the hill is his home
Although he never took a wife, Ronnie leads a gentleman's life
Good transport means a lot to him, the Defender is as good as kin
The power is there as Ronnie knows, his lane's no problem in the snow
To church, to town, the mart, no matter where,
The Defender takes Ronnie everywhere

Take my advice and heed away, on a never-ending holiday
But knowing you as we do, farming is in the blood and part of you
If Sammy rings and wants a hand, Ronnie says, 'I'm your man'
There's silage to haul, sheep to the mart,
Malcolm's ready to make a start

A special virtue you do possess, is telling yarns, you do it best
May you continue for many years, everyone listens, we're all ears
Don't let this poem swell your head;
Or the barbaring price will swell instead
May your birthdays never end, goodwill wishes from all your friends.

Edwina McFarland

MY SUMMER NOSTALGIA

What does summer mean to me?
Rays of warming sunshine bright
Sight of seagulls large and white
Gliding o'er sand and sea
As kids an' dogs on beaches run
Screaming, barking, having fun!

Summer welcomes swallows home
O'er distant foam to familiar eaves,
Birds squabble as magpie thieves
Flocking on rose emblazoned lawn,
Amid the buzzing o' inebriate bees
As dancing butterflies sip plants and trees.

I adore croaking frogs in ponds at play,
With plump cooing woodpigeon's song
As cuckoo echoes in woods among;
Blackbird melodies the start an' end of day
And families gaily splash round a busy beach
Cooling hot bodies in quieter water's reach.

Watching trout on river rising to the fly
Ply dragonfly of winged gossamer sheen,
As cattle lay munching sweet verbage green
Gaze at skylark twittering high
While laughing folk with suntan faces
Frisk like visitors from exotic places.

World relaxes in cool attire,
Snoozes peacefully in leafy shade
Sipping cool beers an' lemonade
While summer's days expire
Man rest his languid eye on
Setting orb, red on far horizon.

Ron Deen

FRUITY DESIRES

An apple each day
does indeed keep the doctor away
but variety is the spice of life, so why not try a fruit cocktail.

Spring brings the blossom
but the fruit does not become wholesome
or succulent until summer or autumn when it may be plucked.

A well balanced diet is good
for you. So have fruit cocktail for starters
and milk and honey for desert which leaves a warm, full sensation.

But take heed, melons, pears
and peaches may have different degrees of ripeness,
adjust proportions of the various fruits according to personal taste.

Taste can be subjective,
some like their cocktails with more melon than pear
but as a general rule peaches are always essential.

A little alcohol added liberally
to the cocktail, helps the juices of the fruits to flow more freely,
the proportions thereafter are less critical.

The cocktail is more palatable
when invited to the party, indeed it can be highly enjoyable;
but be warned, gatecrashers are forbidden.

Fruit cocktail can be eaten every
day of the week, but the tastebuds can sometimes be
deadened if it is consumed to excess.

As an alternative for fruit hungry females, a banana longboat;
ice cream with bananas and cherries is a useful desert,
particularly following a first course of Swedish meatballs.

Chris Barnes

MY FRIEND

(Dedicated to Conrad)

Over many years we became one,
Life was wonderful.
Each day looked forward to
Then out of the blue,
With no warning
What once was one had become two.
No one to hold and keep me warm
On a cold winter's night.
Life goes on, this I know
So I went out and bought
A strange little pup,
Yet I will never forget
The great times we shared.
My little brown stained china tea cup.

Tina McAuley

HOLLY

Life is tough when you're a cat like me
You have to be careful not to get stuck up a tree
Those blasted birds are so inconsiderate
You've gone higher and higher before you're aware of it
Then you capture a little mouse, just, to have a play
And what happens? Those blasted humans take it away
Oh dear what more to be said
I think I'll just retire to 'their' bed
I'll dream my dreams and pretend I'm a winner
They'll soon be calling me down for dinner.

Roberta Affleck

THE HOLE

When I was walking down the street
How many people did I meet?
I didn't meet a single soul
Because they all fell down a hole
I didn't fall down the hole you see
I made it up, there was only me.

Joy McFaul (9)

CHUFFIN' SANTA

Where is that chuffin' Santa
with my sack stuffed full of toys?
My stress balls for the office!
My new set of alloys!
I sent my bloomin' order
way back, months ago.
I hope the daft, old codger's
not stuck somewhere in the snow
or wedged up someone's chimney
too fat to wriggle free.
How could the mad, old codger
disappoint a lad like me?
Perhaps his sleigh's got punctures
or Rudolph's ill in bed.
Or perhaps it's true when people say
that chuffin' Santa's dead.

Sandy MacKay

SEVENTY

Not many yearn for the three score and ten,
yet for some it's been here and away.
To me though you see, it's the now, not the when,
for the seventy span is today.

The threshold's attained; the years have flown,
time has melted away like the snows.
But when I think back, had I only but known,
I'd have planned for more highs than lows.

Reflections are good for the soul some believe,
as there's always the good with the bad.
But what I have now and all I receive,
is surely far better than ever I had.

To look forward too much and continually wonder,
is not in keeping with growing old grace.
Much better to ponder, the days 'way back yonder',
than cherish ambition with a crinkled, old face.

The brigade I have joined is the elite of the flock,
its wisdom supreme is the envy of some.
Though still not immune from occasional shock,
I'm telling myself that the best's yet to come.

Yes! We all have a yen for this threshold en masse,
but now mine's arrived, there's something absurd.
It's become nicer to look in the rear window glass,
as the view from the windscreen has suddenly blurred.

But I'm here at last with loved family and friends;
and for living this life we're all keen.
So if we play our cards right and follow the trends,
we might all get congrats from the queen.

W A Mack

JUSTICE?

Why do we only fight on soil
That is rich in thick, black oil?
We make excuses there that we
Have come to set the natives free

From oil-free lands we keep away
And watch their people strive
To free themselves from tyranny
To find food to survive

Our leaders do not seem to care
For oppressed people's rights
If there is no economic gain
They sweep them out of sight

The time has come for us to rise
And humane justice seek
Make nations who are strongest
Start to protect the weak

Regardless of their status
Let us do what is right
Forget the oil beneath the soil
And just for justice fight.

Ian Russell

LIVING MARKET

The gift of life is not a gift, if you're charged for it from birth,
With your age comes a profit and an increase in worth.
Alas that air is the only thing that comes without a price.
But every attempt of power is a rolling of the dice.
Technology advances in a race for greater wealth
Though it's labelled for mankind, our future and our health.
However far away and however far you've gone,
You'll still be taxed for living, regardless if it's wrong.
For man is governed by some men consumed by their greed
Driven by desires and not by what they need.
Politics is strange when it comes to good ideas,
They justify their percentage for its poverty they fear,
Where are all accomplishment, achievement and glory?
Perhaps upon a mantle in the custody of Tory,
If all the money in all the earth was given just to you
Would you consider it a bargain, when the pound of flesh is due?
The Devil has a price for each of us in turn,
Do you offer him your soul? or let the b****** burn?

Jason L Wolf

A KING'S RANSOM

Today the cost of living's high,
You must agree:
For fifty quid, the things you buy
You'd hardly see.

From wage of two pounds - princely fee!
In fifty-one,
My pocket money bought for me
Bagfuls of fun.

At flicks, be-bop or other meets,
Week after week,
We'd bubble gum or suck hard sweets,
Glued cheek to cheek.

Such simple, guileless rendezvous
We'd daily chart,
When chips, steam-wrapped in last week's news
Was *a la carte.*

On weekends then my heart would sing,
Out on the town,
With ransom fit for modest king:
A half-a-crown.

J R Parkes

UNTITLED

An angel being of light, came and sat on my right
He spoke a word, I've never heard
And gave me such a fright.

But lo and behold, the story he told
Was of love divine, soon to be mine
Even though I was getting old

'Prepare yourself,' he spoke aloud, 'you must stand out from the crowd
Look your best, for this test
Even at 50, love is still allowed.'

I asked, 'Are you sure? I'm not exactly pure
I've lived my life, I'm no longer a wife
My condition - divorce - there is no cure.'

'Alas, I tell you, have no fear, this love is meant my dear
He's rich and tall, you'll have a ball
He looks like Jeremy from Top Gear.'

'Oh please hurry, I just can't wait, go and fetch my handsome date
Get your friends to clear his path, I'll go and have a bath
I feel so dreamy this must be fate.'

So I bathed and dressed to please, trying not to look a tease
It's all very well being witty, but another thing being pretty
I don't know a plastic surgeon who has no fees.

Here he comes, my angel friend, I hear his wings rustle and bend
My eyes pop, and I nearly choke, what a lovely, sexy bloke
His taste in men I must commend.

I walk towards this gorgeous beefcake, purse my lips, a kiss to take
Fluttering hard my one eyelash, whoosh, he's gone in a flash
Crash, on the floor, I'm now awake.

Eleanor Morgan

ARMAGEDDON NOW

I listened to the words
There is no reality here
My sleep is interrupted
The dream, a fog-filled blur.

The picture is distorted
I know I must awake
No such reality exists
Can this horror be aborted?

I defy the existence
The depths of depravity
Cannot be of this world
Yet the voice is insistent.

I am forced to acknowledge this calamity
A new depth has been reached
And a new dimension is born.
Not just inhumanity

Armageddon now
Is surely justified
To erase such evil
That lives in human souls.

C O Burnell

MEMORIES OF WAR

On Christmas Day I'll be eighty-five
If God in His grace let's me live
These last days have suddenly revealed
I may have something to give,

Memories of a market garden
Cutting flowers at 7am and then
Weighing fruit already gathered by workers,
Lorry all ready and packed up by ten.

Breakfast in the farmhouse kitchen
With prisoners of war (German they were).
One a doctor, all very mannerly I recall
Joking, laughing, a big meal we'd share.

Tina was with the Land Army
Me? I was only 'doing my bit',
The war still had a long way to go,
The 'blackout' was really . . . a pit!

No torches allowed to show the path,
Countryside was dark - like the towns
Bombers would find us - death beckoned
But faces were smiling - no frowns.

There have always been wars, and rumours of wars.
All through my travels you see
But today they came, the memories,
Next year? Whatever will be, will be.

Alice Carlin

MYRA

She's gone then, whisper her name.
Though none would envy her claim to fame.

At her demise; few shed a tear.
Look over your shoulder with a frisson of fear.

An unnatural woman, a beast of her times
Heaven abhorred her unspeakable crimes.

Marjory Gordon

NO SOUND FROM PICTURES

Flicking through the brochures, it is a time of cheer,
Deciding where you'll end up on holiday next year.
Pictures all look marvellous, with views that will astound,
One thing they can't relay to you, is noise that's all around.
The day comes round; excitement banishes all the gloom,
Before you know you're on the plane then shown to your room.
The day has seemed too very long and on your body taxing,
Looking forward to the time ahead, totally relaxing.
Because of all the travelling you have an early night,
So you'll wake up next day, refreshed from that long flight.
As head rests down on pillow, where dreamland should be found,
Your ears become alerted to all the nightmare sound.
The walls as thin as paper, the ceiling seems to bounce,
Noise comes from all directions to on your hearing pounce.
The window was left open to circulate the air,
What pictures couldn't tell you of nightclubs and just where?
Clubbers around prepare themselves for a riotous night ahead,
Due to the thinness of the walls, you hear every word that's said.
From talking up to shouting, all laughing and the hoots,
Then marching on the ceiling with what seems like hobnail boots.
It goes on till almost dawn when music and neons fade,
Clubbers then return to rooms like soldiers out on raids.
They clatter up the staircase, the doors crash in their sockets,
Crashing for a second time to make sure that they lock it.
Water then runs constant as taps and toilet flushes,
It sounds like Niagara Falls as down the pipes it rushes.
With morning nearly on us, we hardly slept a wink,
Only time our eyes were shut; when bright lights made us blink.
The only thing in favour that helps us keep our cool,
Is knowing during daylight we may sleep by the pool.

Jim Fraser

CHILDREN OF WAR

Little children of a world in peace long ago
Frolicking and playing with their cheeks all aglow
In a world where they lived in a peaceful domain
Where all that was promising was theirs to attain!

When did our children's hopes turn to dust?
When did they lose their innocence and trust?
Their carefree joy had gone, their bubble had burst
All the things they believed in, it seemed was cursed

All the good things in life and all their serenity
Had disappeared like that of a wedding's confetti
Their dreams of a fine future like grains of flung rice
Had gone, to a senseless war they had paid the price

The bloated ambitions of a dictator's warfare
The misguided armies of humanity's despair
Piles of dead flesh and the cries of those left
Heartbroken loved ones at home and bereft

Now clearing up after the frenzy had died
Those sacrifices which could not be denied
To right the wrongs of the weapons that were hurled
As they tried to make sense of a muddled world

Now a new war is raging from a different beast
A new madness is fighting us from the Middle East
Our soldiers, while battling with those they can see
Are hampered by the suicidal bombers running free

Oh! why can't the black-hearted despots be caught?
Before they've had time to make the world distraught!
We need the retribution of a wrathful God
To make the earth we live on more safe to be trod.

Royston E Herbert

DROWNING DARKNESS

Dawn silhouettes the mountain drapes
shadows over the sunken valley as
dawn splashes the tips of the rugged peaks orange.

Fluid daylight cascades down dry gullies
in rippling pinpoints of light
scintillating spectrums in the morning dew.

Rapidly the valley floods
higher than the water
deeper than the dam.

Hamish Lee

FOUNDATIONS OF FRUSTRATION

Visible panty lines (VPL)
Where have they gone
Have they become invisible
Or are they just not in
Vogue

Evidence of underwear amiss
So perhaps none is worn
Imagine a suited lady seated
In brave 'commando' mode
Trouser seams start to split
A body in two halves right
Up to the dimpled chin
Spliced. Extremely not nice
Face it girls - as we grimace
Our sensitive areas are no longer
A private matter

Foundation garments . . .
Lingerie language is well-known
But not outlined and shown
French knickers
Thongs
G-strings
Bikinis
Minis
High legs
The list could go on . . .
But I fear this brief ode
May end up too risky

Theresa Mead

MIND BENDER

In nightclubbing, night hugging
Decadence she revels,
Glitzy and ritzy, sways, sensuous,
Through jagged eyes of 'E' swirling;
Shrill in the momentum
Circles her voice;
Keepers of peace loom large,
Menacing; laughter echoes, echoes,
In the cavern of her mind,
Shadows unveil, kaleidoscope revealed;
The past recedes, desperate, into
The future; as transient night
Steals out to waiting dawn,
Life's shroud,
Collected at the door.

Dorothy Neil

So Close To Silence

You may not hear the footsteps walk behind you
but I know you feel the presence in your soul,
my speech may be so close to silence
but the spirit of my voice is your control
that leads each small vibration to the doorway, where your mind
absorbs the aural energy and translates each spoken line.

So as I shape and form my words, I begin to realise
that sounds transmit emotions that are written in the eyes.
Bared for all the world to see, naked on the sands,
to be stored and reinterpreted by the clever use of hands,
that sign each vowel and consonant, to allow you to reply
with light-hearted comments, to your friend who stands nearby,

who understands each gesture and the emotions they contain
so that the body's feelings are taken to a higher plane.
Where springtime turns to summer, life's garden starts to bloom
excitement, turns to energy and brightens up our room.
Our conversation dances with eloquence and flair
without discrimination, but with tender loving care.

So that who we are is focused on, not what we can and cannot do
judged by disability's a myopic point of view,
that's destined to be abandoned, to be left and cast aside
forever as the bridesmaid; to never be the bride
who stands proud at the alter with her family and friends,
she's surrounded by the senses that lack of hearing so depends.

Each footstep leaves impressions and raises questions on the way
but the common bond of love we share leaves a spiritual bouquet,
that lifts the mist of misconception that those who cannot hear
somehow are disabled and devoid of new ideas,
that their value and potential remains forever undisclosed
but it's all just an illusion that rarely gets exposed.

Alan Glendinning

INFORMATION

We hope you have enjoyed reading this book - and that you will continue to enjoy it in the coming years.

If you like reading and writing poetry drop us a line, or give us a call, and we'll send you a free information pack.

Alternatively if you would like to order further copies of this book or any of our other titles, then please give us a call or log onto our website at www.forwardpress.co.uk

Anchor Books Information
Remus House
Coltsfoot Drive
Peterborough
PE2 9JX
(01733) 898102